PRIMITIVE CHURCH OFFICES.

ESSAYS

ON THE

PRIMITIVE CHURCH OFFICES.

REPRINTED BY PERMISSION FROM THE PRINCETON REVIEW, WITH CORRECTIONS AND ADDITIONS BY THE SAME WRITER.

NEW-YORK:
CHARLES SCRIBNER, 145 NASSAU-STREET.
1851.

JOHN. F. TROW,
Printer and Stereotyper,
49 Ann-Street.

ADVERTISEMENT.

THE essays here collected were originally published in different numbers of the Biblical Repertory and Princeton Review during a period of several years. A desire having been expressed for their republication in a separate form, the author has not only given his consent, but made a number of corrections, chiefly verbal, and two additions of considerable length, to wit, the whole of the fifth essay and the conclusion of the fourth, comprising the argument in reference to the apostleship of Titus. Both these additions formed a part of the original manuscript, from which the essays were transferred to the Review, and are necessary to complete the argument. An occasional want of uniformity in the use of the singular and plural pronoun has arisen from a partial restoration of the original form, which was afterwards abandoned, as a superfluous labour in a mere republication.

CONTENTS.

ESSAY I.

ON THE ORIGIN OF THE CHRISTIAN ELDERSHIP.

In various living languages there are titles of honour and respect, the etymological origin of which is to be sought in the idea of old age or seniority. Such are *Sire*, as addressed to kings, and the cognate expression *Sir*, as used in common parlance, and also in the title of an English knight or baronet. Such too are the French *Sieur*, *Seigneur*, the Spanish *Señor*, the Italian *Signore*, with their various compounds, *Monsieur*, *Monseigneur*, *Monsignore*, *Messire*, etc., all which may be traced back to the Latin *Senior*, considered as the comparative of *Senex*. We find, moreover, that terms thus derived have been extensively employed, not only as expressions of personal respect, but also as designations of official dignity. This is the case with most of the words already mentioned, to which may be added *Alderman* (elder man), *Senator*, *Patres Conscripti*, the Arabic *Sheikh*, and many others.

This extensive use of words, which properly denote

old age, to signify official rank, might possibly admit of explanation on the hypothesis, that what was first used to express a merely personal respect was afterwards employed to express the same feeling with respect to public or official dignity; that as any respected person might be called a father or an old man, so a ruler or a magistrate might be so called by way of eminence. But the usage now in question may be still more satisfactorily accounted for, by the fact, that as we trace the history of governments backwards, we find them all to terminate in the patriarchal system. It is this which exists in families among all nations. It is founded on the natural relation between parents and children. It has no concern with artificial theories respecting social compacts and equality. Among those races which have retained most of a primitive simplicity in their mode of life, this organization of society is still found. As the father governs his own household, so the head of the family, i. e. of the elder branch, governs the younger, and the head of the whole tribe governs both. This system lingers still among the Highland clans of Scotland, and continues in full force among the wandering Arabs. Hence their strict regard to genealogy, which existed also among the ancient Hebrews.

Under all the changes in the Hebrew form of government, this patriarchal system still remained as the substratum of the whole theocracy; and its peculiar phraseology is constantly recurring in the sacred history. As the natural heads of houses, families, and tribes, were the hereditary magistrates, the name זְקֵנִים, *old men, elders*, was the common appellation for the rulers of the people.

The same usage of the term occurs in application to domestic arrangements. Eliezer of Damascus, Abraham's steward, is called (Gen. 24 : 2) עַבְדּוֹ זְקַן בֵּיתוֹ, not "his eldest servant of his house," as our translation has it, but "his servant, the elder (i. e. ruler) of his house." So in Gen. 50 : 7, we read of "all the servants of Pharaoh, the elders of his house," as well as "all the elders of the land of Egypt." These *elders* and the *senators* of Ps. 105 : 22 are identical in Hebrew.

During the residence of Israel in Egypt, the patriarchal system seems to have been maintained, as one suited to every change of circumstances. Hence, when the people were to be delivered, the communications from Jehovah were made, not directly to the mass of the nation, but to the Elders, as their national and acknowledged representatives. When God commanded Moses (Ex. 3 : 14), "Thus shalt thou say unto the children of Israel, I AM hath sent me unto you," he immediately explained the way in which the command was to be executed, by adding, "Go and gather THE ELDERS of Israel together, and say unto them," etc. (v. 16), "and thou shalt come, thou and THE ELDERS of Israel, unto the king of Egypt" (v. 18). Again we read (Ex. 4 : 30, 31), that Moses and Aaron "did the signs in the sight of THE PEOPLE, and THE PEOPLE believed." But immediately before it had been said (v. 29), that they "went and gathered together all THE ELDERS of the children of Israel," which would be a nugatory statement, if it did not mean that the *people,* who saw the signs and believed in consequence, were the *elders of the people.*

In Ex. 12 : 3, the Lord says unto Moses and Aaron, "Speak ye unto *all the congregation* of Israel;" but in executing this command "Moses called for all *the elders* of Israel," and gave them the necessary orders (v. 21). When Moses smote the rock by divine direction, it was "in the sight of the elders of Israel" (Ex. 17 : 5, 6), as the representatives of the people who were to be relieved, and at the same time reproved for murmuring. When Jethro offered sacrifices and made a feast, "all the elders of Israel" came, as a matter of course, "to eat bread with Moses' father-in-law before God" (Ex. 18 : 12).

A still more remarkable instance of the Elders being taken for the people is in Ex. 19 : 8, where it is said that "ALL THE PEOPLE answered together and said, all that the Lord hath spoken we will do; and Moses told the words of THE PEOPLE unto the Lord;" whereas in the verse immediately preceding it is said, that "Moses came and called for THE ELDERS of the people, and laid before their faces all these words which the Lord commanded him." Another example of the same thing may be found in Deut. 5 : 23, where Moses, addressing the people, says, "Ye came near unto me, (even) all the heads of your tribes and your elders."

In the Mosaic ritual, the Elders are recognized as the representatives of the people, not only by being joined with Aaron and his sons in the directions with respect to certain sacrifices (Lev. 9 : 1), but in the solemn ceremony of imposing hands upon the victim, as a symbol of the transfer of the sins of the whole people to the substitute (Lev. 4 : 15).

The "seventy elders" (Num. 11 : 25), who acted as assistants to Moses and Aaron in certain cases, were not ordained to a new office, but merely selected for a special purpose from a body of men already in existence. They are expressly called "seventy of the elders" (Ex. 24 : 1), "seventy men of the elders of Israel, whom thou knowest to be the elders of the people and officers set over them" (Num. 11 : 16). Nothing could more clearly intimate the previous existence and official standing of the elders. In this case it is plain that the word "officers" is in apposition with "elders" and explanatory of it, a remark which admits of a very extensive and important application.

The use of the same term in reference to other nations, if it does not prove that the same natural and simple organization obtained among them, proves what is more important, that the Hebrew writers were so perfectly familiar with this government by Elders, and this representation of the people by their Elders, that they naturally used expressions borrowed from it, to describe the institutions of other countries. In Num. 22 : 4, we read that "Moab said unto the Elders of Midian," which might seem to imply a difference of organization; but that *Moab* means the *Elders of Moab*, appears from v. 7, where we find the full phrase, "and the Elders of Moab and the Elders of Midian departed." In Joshua 9 : 11, the Gibeonites describe their rulers by the name of Elders.

In the laws of Moses which have a prospective reference to the settlement of the people in the promised land, he mentions not only the Elders of Israel collectively (Lev. 4 : 15, Num. 11 : 16) and the Elders of the several tribes (Deut. 31 : 28. 29 : 10), but the Elders of cities and districts, who are represented as the local magistrates or judges (Deut. 19 : 12. 21 : 2, 3, 4, 6, 19. 22 : 15–18. 25 : 7–9).

The Elders are joined with Aaron in the receiving

of the law (Lev. 9 : 1), and with Moses in the giving of it (Deut. 27 : 1). In like manner we find Joshua accompanied by the Elders in certain public acts (Josh. 7 : 6. 8 : 10).. In those cases where the people *en masse* were to bear a part, the Elders still appear as their official leaders (Josh. 8 : 33. 23 : 2. 24 : 1), though in some of the cases here referred to, it is doubtful whether any other assembling of the people was intended or possible than that of a representative nature. In Josh. 23 : 2, for example, we may either read "the people and their elders," or "the people even (viz.) their elders."

That the government by Elders still existed after the conquest of Canaan, is evident from history. When Gideon dealt with the people of Succoth, it was in the person of their Elders (Judg. 8 : 16); Jephthah's negotiations were with the Elders of Gilead (Judg. 11 : 5–11); and at the very close of the book of Judges we find the "Elders of the congregation," i. e. of the whole church and nation, deliberating jointly on a matter which concerned their relations to a single tribe (Judg. 21 : 16).

The local Elders seem to have been numerous. Those of Succoth were in number seventy-seven, as appears from Judges 8 : 14, where Elders and Princes (i. e. rulers, chiefs) are in apposition, and descriptive of one office. The Elders of the people are again mentioned, Ruth 4 : 4. The influence of the Elders in withstanding the progress of corruption, after the death of Moses and Joshua, is twice expressly recorded (Josh. 24 : 31. Judges 2 : 7).

In the time of Samuel, we still meet with occasional

allusions to the Elders of cities (e. g. Jabesh, 1 Sam. 11: 3, and Bethlehem ch. 16 : 4), the Elders of tribes (e. g. Judah, 1 Sam. 30: 26), and the Elders of all Israel, as the collective rulers of the nation, who made war and peace (1 Sam. 4: 3), changed the external form of government (8: 4), to whom even Samuel listened with respect (ib.), and of whose contempt even Saul was afraid (15: 30). The circumstances attending the introduction of monarchy show clearly that the change was a formal one, and that after as before it the details of the government continued in the hands of the hereditary Elders.

During the reigns of David and Solomon, we find the most important questions of government (as, for example, who should be king) repeatedly referred to, and decided by, the Elders of Israel (2 Sam. 3: 17. 5: 3, 1 Chron. 11: 3) and Judah (2 Sam. 19: 11). When Absalom usurped his father's throne, it was with the connivance of the Elders of Israel (2 Sam. 17: 4, 15). When Solomon was about to remove the ark, he assembled the Elders of Israel, i. e. "the heads of the tribes, the chiefs of the fathers of the children of Israel;" for these words are to be regarded as explanatory of the title *elders* (1 Kings 8: 1, 3. 2 Chron. 5: 2, 4). The officers of David's palace are called the Elders of his house (2 Sam. 12: 17). That the king was commonly attended by Elders as counsellors and aids, may be gathered from such incidental statements as that in 1 Chr. 15: 25. 21: 16.

Solomon himself alludes to this organization when, describing the husband of the virtuous woman, he says, "her husband is known in the gate, when he sitteth among the Elders of the land" (Prov. 31: 23).

Isaiah mentions the Elder, in enumerating the public persons who were to be removed from Judah (Isa. 3 : 2. 9 : 14). He describes Jehovah's controversy with his people as carried on against "the Elders, even the rulers, of the people," as their representatives. In predicting the future glory of the church, or of Jehovah in the church, he says, "The Lord shall reign in Mount Zion, and in Jerusalem, and before his Elders, gloriously" (Isa. 24:23).

After the revolt of the ten tribes, the government by Elders still subsisted in both kingdoms. When Benhadad, king of Syria, sent an overbearing message to Ahab, king of Israel, the latter "called all the Elders of the land," and acted by their counsel (1 Kings 20 : 7, 8). When the same king wished to obtain Naboth's vineyard, Jezebel procured the death of Naboth by her influence over "the Elders and the nobles" (or even the nobles) "that were in his city" (1 Kings 21 : 8).

The practice of regarding the elders as the people, in all public acts, still appears in such expressions as "the men of his city, even the elders and the nobles that were in his city" (1 Kings 21 : 11), and in the statement that Josiah "went up into the house of the Lord, and ALL THE MEN OF JUDAH, and the inhabitants of Jerusalem, and the priests and levites, and ALL THE PEOPLE, great and small" (2 Kings 23 : 2. 2 Chron. 34 : 30). Strictly understood, this was impossible. It is not, however, a mere synecdoche or hyperbole. It does not mean that *some* of the people went up, which would not account for the strength of the expressions. The whole people, great and small, were really present, according to the principle of representation. They were present in the person of their Elders, for we read in 2 Kings 23 : 1 (2 Chron. 34 : 29), that "the king sent, and they gathered unto him ALL THE ELDERS of Judah and Jerusalem." The existence of local Elders, during this same period, may be inferred, not only from the case of Naboth above mentioned, but from the incidental statements, that "Elisha sat in his house, and the Elders sat with him" (2 Kings 6 : 32); and that "Jehu wrote letters, and sent to Samaria, unto the rulers of Jezreel, the Elders" (2 Kings 10 : 1). In this last case, the identity of the *rulers* and *elders* is unusually clear from the omission of the copulative, which shows that when the particle appears in other cases of the same kind, it is not distinctive but explanatory. The official existence and activity of Elders may be traced to the very end of the kingdom of Judah, as we find "the elders of the land," in the reign of Jehoiakim, interposing in behalf of Jeremiah (Jer. 26 : 17).

One advantage of this presbyterial constitution was, that being founded upon natural relations, it could exist wherever families existed; and we find accordingly that, as it was maintained during the long sojourn of Israel in Egypt, so the Elders were still recognized, as a distinct order, in the Babylonish exile, as appears from "the letter that Jeremiah the Prophet sent from Jerusalem unto the residue of THE ELDERS which were carried away captive," etc. (Jer. 29 : 1). So, likewise, when the exiles applied to Ezekiel for information as to the will of God, it was through their Elders (Ezek. 20 : 1, 3). When he was transported in vision to Jerusalem, he was made to see the abominations committed by "the Elders of the house of Israel"

(Ezek. 8 : 12); and at the very time when the trance fell upon him he was sitting, like Elisha, in his house, and "the Elders of Judah" sat before him (ib. v. 1).

And as the official rank of the Elders was still recognized during the captivity, so it re-appears after the return from exile. The decrees made were "according to the counsel of the Princes and the Elders" (Ezra 10 : 8), or, as we have seen that this construction probably means, "the Chiefs, to wit, the Elders." The combination is intended to show that the chiefs referred to were not temporary or extraordinary ones, but such as held power under the ancient theocratical constitution. So in Ezra 10 : 14, where the "Rulers (or Elders) of all the congregation" are distinguished from "the Elders of every city and the Judges thereof," the last phrase seems to be exegetical of the former, and intended to show that the Elders of each city were its local magistrates, which, as we have seen already, was the ancient Hebrew polity.

The "Elders of the Priests," who are occasionally mentioned (Isa. 37 : 2. 2 Kings 19 : 2), appear to have been the heads of the several branches of the family of Aaron, the same who in the New Testament are called ἀρχιερεῖς or Chief Priests. In Jer. 19 : 1, they are distinguished from the "Elders of the people," i. e. of the other tribes.

This organization was for religious as well as civil purposes. Hence the Psalmist says, "Praise him in the assembly of the Elders" (Ps. 107 : 32). Indeed, the whole organization of the Hebrew commonwealth was for a religious purpose. The nation was the church. The same chiefs who presided over secular affairs, presided over sacred things, except that what related to ceremonial matters was intrusted to the chiefs of a single tribe exclusively. Sacrifice and all that pertained to it was under the direction of the Priests at the tabernacle or temple; but when the people met elsewhere for spiritual worship, it was under the direction of their natural and ordinary chiefs, the Elders. These meetings were in later times called *συναγωγαί*, a name which was sometimes extended to the houses in which they were held.

This view of the matter relieves the question as to the antiquity of synagogues from much of its difficulty. The common opinion is, that they arose during the captivity, when the people had no access to the temple. But the temple-service and that of the synagogue were totally distinct. The one could not be a succedaneum for the other. If the want of a local spiritual worship was felt during the exile, it must have been felt centuries before. It seems incredible that, during a course of ages, those who could not attend the temple were without any stated worship. The argument urged in favour of this doctrine is, that synagogues are not mentioned before the captivity. But this proceeds upon the supposition, that the ancient synagogue was a distinct organization within the body politic, an *imperium in imperio.* The difficulty vanishes as soon as we assume, that it was nothing but the stated meeting of the people, under their national organization, for a particular purpose, the worship of God. It was a civil organization used for a religious purpose; or rather, it was one organization, used both for a religious and a civil purpose; as in England the *parishes* are both ecclesiastical and political divisions of the kingdom. The same state of things would exist among us, if the townships met statedly for public worship, under the same moderators and committees who are charged with the conduct of their secular affairs. These officers would answer to the Jewish Elders. Under such a system, church and state would not only be united but identified, as they were in the Hebrew commonwealth. The Jewish church was the Jewish nation, and the same persons were church-officers and magistrates. The instruction of the people, and perhaps the conduct of religious worship, were probably intrusted to the Levites, who, when not on actual duty at Jerusalem, lived dispersed among the people. From this tribe probably proceeded most of the Scribes, Lawyers, or Doctors of the Law, which seem to have been titles, not of an office, but of a profession, the business of which was to expound the Scriptures, and perhaps to take the lead in public worship. But the legal authority, in these as well as other things, resided in the Elders of the several communities, who, in relation to their spiritual functions were called *Elders* or *Rulers of the Synagogue.*

This state of things still continued when Christ came. The people were still governed by their Elders, both in civil and religious matters. Collectively, the Elders are called *Elders of the People* (Matthew 21:23. 26:3), and *Elders of the Jews* (Luke 7:3), and are continually joined with the *Chief Priests* (or Elders of the Priests), in all the public acts with reference to the arrest, trial, condemnation, and crucifixion of our Lord (Matt. 16:21. 26:47, 59. 27:1, 3, 12. 28:12, etc). Peter and John were arraigned before the *Elders of Israel* (Acts 4:8, 23); Stephen was condemned by them (Acts 6:12); Paul was persecuted by them

(Acts 23 : 14), and by them accused before the Roman governor (Acts 24 : 1. 25 : 15).

There seems to be no doubt, then, that the government by Elders, which we have seen to be coeval with the commonwealth, and to have survived all political changes, continued until the destruction of the temple and dispersion of the people.

Our Lord began his ministry by exhorting men to repent because the kingdom of heaven was at hand. In this he was preceded by John the Baptist, and followed by the twelve disciples whom he sent out for the purpose, "whom also he named *Apostles*" (Luke 6 : 13). That which they all preached or proclaimed was *the gospel of the kingdom* (Matt. 4 : 23. 9 : 35. 24 : 14. Mark 1 : 14), i. e. the good news that a kingdom was about to be established. That this new kingdom was not to be merely inward and spiritual, is clear from what is said as to the personal distinctions and diversities of ranks which were to have place in it (Matt. 5 : 19. 11 : 11. 18 : 4). If the kingdom of heaven merely meant an inward state, in what sense could one be greater than another as a subject of that kingdom ? Such expressions necessarily imply that it denotes an outward state of things, and that not merely a condition of society, but a society itself. It was called a kingdom, not merely because the hearts and lives of men were to be governed by new principles, but because they were to be brought, even externally, under a new *régime*, an organized government. True, the spiritual nature of this government is also asserted. Christ himself declared, that his kingdom was not of this world (John 18 : 36), and Paul tells the Romans that "the kingdom of God is not meat and drink, but righteousness and peace and joy in the Holy Ghost" (Rom. 14 : 17). Our Lord himself, on being asked when the kingdom of God should come, answered, "the kingdom of God cometh not *μετὰ παρατηρήσεως*," in a striking and sensible manner; "for," he adds, "the kingdom of God is within you" (Luke 17 : 21). All these expressions were intended to guard against the opposite extreme of considering the kingdom of God as something merely external, and to direct attention to those spiritual changes which were necessarily involved in the true doctrine of the kingdom. The very design of its establishment was spiritual. It was to exercise authority in the hearts of men. Hence, unless it did affect their hearts, it mattered not what outward signs of its approach were visible. Unless it was within them, it could not possibly exist without them, or rather they could have no part in its advantages. It did not follow from this, however, that it existed only within them, any more than it followed, from the necessity of faith to give efficacy to sacrifices, that there was no need of the outward rite at all. The kingdom of God was an outward institution for a spiritual purpose. It was to be as really a kingdom as the kingdom of David or of Herod. Was it then to take the place of the old system, as of something wholly different in kind? Not at all. It was merely to succeed it, as the end succeeds the beginning, as maturity succeeds infancy and youth. The Jews were already under a theocracy. God was their king in a peculiar sense. He did not merely rule them, as he does all nations, with a providential sway. He filled that place in their political system which is filled in other states by human sovereigns. Jerusalem was his capital, and the temple there his palace. This was still the case during all the outward changes in the form of government. But this system was a temporary one. It had been predicted, that the time was coming when God should reign, not only over the Jews, but in all parts of the earth, not under the forms of any national organization, but independently of the kingdoms of the world. The restrictions of the ancient theocracy were to be done away. This was the kingdom which our Lord announced, and for which he called upon the people to prepare by reformation and repentance, an organized system of government distinct from all secular establishments, in other words a *church.*

The Jews who used the Greek language were perfectly familiar with the word *ἐκκλησία* from its frequent occurrence in the Septuagint as an equivalent to קָהָל, one of the Hebrew terms denoting the whole congregation of Israel. It was not merely a collective name for many dispersed individuals having a common character or faith or practice, but a defined body, a distinct society, *called out* from the world at large, *called together* for a special purpose, and possessing within itself an organization for the attainment of that purpose. Such was the church of the Old Testament. The Jewish nation was set apart for a peculiar purpose, and received a peculiar organization with reference to that purpose. The identity of this church with the church of the New Testament may be argued from the identity of their design, which was, in either case, to preserve and perpetuate divine truth, to maintain public worship, and promote spiritual edification by means of discipline, mutual communion, and a common participation in the same advantages. These ends were attained in different ways under the two systems. What was prospective in the one was retrospective in the other. Christ was the end of the law and the beginning of the gospel. Both pointed to him, though in different directions; but as to their main design and fundamental principles, they were the same. Our Lord came not to destroy but to fulfil. He came not so much to institute a new church, as to give a new organization to the old, or rather to prepare the way for such a re-organization; which did not take place, and was not meant to take place, during his personal ministry.

This is evident, 1. From the absence of any intimation, expressed or implied, of such organization. There is no account given in the gospels of the formation of societies, or the creation of any officers, except the twelve and the seventy, who were sent out with precisely the same powers. The only difference is this, that we hear no more of the seventy, from which we may infer, that they were appointed for a temporary purpose, perhaps to spread the first annunciation of the kingdom more extensively than the twelve could do it, although the latter body was sufficiently numerous for all its ulterior functions.

2. The appointment of these ministers does not imply an actual organization of the Christian church, because they were originally appointed, and during their Lord's presence upon earth employed, as the announcers of a state of things which was still in prospect. We have seen that our Lord and his forerunner called men to repent, because the kingdom of heaven

was at hand. To provide assistants and successors in this great work of announcing the new state of things, he began to select persons who should attend him for that purpose. Of the persons thus gradually gathered, six are particularly mentioned in the course of the narrative, namely, Andrew, Peter, James, John, Philip, and Matthew. When the number amounted to twelve, they were formed into a body and invested with official powers. The remaining six were Bartholomew, Thomas, James the son of Alpheus, Lebbeus or Thaddeus, Simon the Canaanite, and Judas Iscariot. These twelve are expressly said to have been appointed "that they might be with him, and that he might send them forth" (Mark 3: 14). Their duties then were twofold, to be with Christ that they might learn, and to go from him that they might teach. In the one case they were μαθηταί, in the other ἀπόστολοι. They first remained with him as disciples, and then went forth as apostles. Hence they are sometimes called "the twelve disciples" (Matt. 10: 1. 11: 1. 20: 17. Luke 9: 1), and even the indefinite expression "the disciples" sometimes means the twelve exclusively (Matt. 12: 1. 13: 10, 36. Mark 11: 14). One of these states was preparatory to the other. They were disciples in order that they might become apostles. They remained with Christ to learn how they must act when they should go forth from him. When they did go forth, it was to announce the approach of the new dispensation, the re-organization of the church, or, as they expressed it, the coming of the kingdom of God. This was their office, to which their other powers were subsidiary. Their preaching was not so much doctrinal instruction as the announcement of approaching changes. Their work was to excite attention and direct it to the proper object. To aid them in so doing, and to attest the authority by which they acted, they were empowered to work miracles of healing. They were also inspired, at least for purposes of self-defence when publicly accused. They were thus commissioned as co-workers with their Lord in the work of introducing the new dispensation and preparing for the re-organization of the church. But these very facts imply that it was not yet re-organized.

3. The same thing is evident from the omission of the name by which the body, after its re-organization, is invariably called. This word (ἐκκλησία), which according to Greek usage signifies an aggregate assembly of the people for municipal purposes, is the term applied, as we have seen, in the Septuagint version, to the whole Jewish church or congregation. In the New Testament it is applied (with some apparent reference to the peculiar use of καλέω and κλῆσις in the sense of calling so as to elect and qualify) to the original body of believers at Jerusalem, and then to the whole body of believers in the world, considered as forming an organized society, and also by a natural synecdoche to bodies of Christians in particular places, as component parts or subdivisions of the whole church. In all these senses the word is familiarly employed in the Acts and Epistles, whereas in the Gospels it occurs but twice, and then, as it should seem, in a prospective application. The first is in the memorable address to Peter: "Thou art Peter, and on this rock will I build my church" (Matt. 16: 18). Without adverting here to the vexed question whether Peter was the rock, and if so, in what sense the church was to be built

upon him, it is plain, from the very form of the expression (*οἰκοδομήσω*), that the founding of the church is spoken of as an event still future. The other case is in our Lord's directions as to the proper mode of dealing with private offenders. "If thy brother trespass against thee, tell it to the church" (Matt. 18: 17). If this means a Christian body then in existence, why is it nowhere else recognized or called by the same name in the gospel history? If not, it must either mean the Jewish church then in existence, or the Christian church yet to be organized. From this it would seem to be at least highly probable, that there was no re-organization of the church during the period of the gospel history.

4. The same thing is evident from the many instances in which our Lord tells his disciples what *shall be* in the kingdom of heaven, as a state of things still future.

5. It is also evident from the manifest ignorance of the apostles as to the details of the re-organization, their gross mistakes, and their frequent inquiries, often betraying an entire misconception of the nature of Christ's kingdom.

6. Closely connected with the proof just stated is the consideration, that the twelve, though qualified to be the announcers of the kingdom, were as yet unqualified to be its rulers. Their notions, as to their Lord's character and person, were confused and erroneous. Their views were narrow; they were full of Jewish prejudices; they were slow of heart to understand and believe the Scriptures; they were selfish and ambitious; they were envious and jealous. This is the picture drawn by inspiration, and among the pens

employed were two of their own number. The whole account is that of persons in a state of pupilage, set apart for a work, with which they were only partially acquainted, and for which they were yet to be prepared. Witness their consternation and amazement when their Lord was taken from them, and the various instances in which it is recorded that the simplest truths were understood by them after his resurrection from the dead. Nor is this unfavourable view contradicted by the fact of their inspiration, which appears to have been limited to a special purpose, as we know that their power of working miracles was not a discretionary power. (See Matt. 17: 16.) When our Lord rose from the dead, his first address to the eleven was in the language of rebuke (Mark 16: 14). He then reassured them and enlarged their powers. He gave them indeed no new powers, but commissioned them to exercise those which they possessed already on a larger scale. At first they were commanded to go neither to the Greeks nor the Samaritans, but only to the Jews. Now they are commissioned to go into all the earth and preach the gospel to every creature (Mark 16: 15). At first they were sent out to announce the coming of God's kingdom to the Jews, now to the Gentiles also. The removal of this restriction marks the beginning of the new dispensation. As long as the gospel of the kingdom was sent only to the Jews, the old economy was still in force, and there was no room for a new organization.

7. The commission to baptize (Matt. 28: 19) was not a new one. This they had done before (John 3: 26. 4: 1, 2), as an expression of readiness, on the part of the baptized, to take part in the kingdom of God,

when it should be set up. But that this rite was not considered as implying that the kingdom was set up already, is clear from the anxious question, asked by the eleven, at the very moment of their Lord's ascension, "Lord, wilt thou, at this time, restore again the kingdom to Israel?" (Acts 1: 6). It is clear from this inquiry, that they had not even formed a just conception of the nature of the kingdom, in which they were to be rulers; how much more that they had not already witnessed its erection.

8. In reply to the question just referred to, Christ does not tell them that the kingdom was restored already, but tacitly admits that it was yet to come. "It is not for you to know the times or the seasons which the Father has put in his own power; but ye shall receive power when the Holy Ghost is come upon you; and ye shall be witnesses unto me, both in Jerusalem and in all Judea, and in Samaria, and unto the uttermost parts of the earth" (Acts 1: 7, 8). Here we have at once the removal of those restrictions which, as we have seen, were inseparable from the old economy, and the promise of that influence by which the twelve were to be qualified to organize the new one. This seems to fix prospectively the date of the actual coming of the kingdom of God, and the organization of the Christian church. Until the day of Pentecost, the apostles and brethren were merely waiting for the kingdom; and it ought to be observed, as a significant coincidence, that the day appointed for the public entrance of the Holy Ghost into the Christian Church, was the same that had been signalized by the formal constitution of the Jewish Church in the promulgation of the law from Sinai.

9. The last proof to be alleged, in favour of the proposition that the church was not re-organized until the day of Pentecost, is furnished by the subsequent change in the character and conduct of the twelve apostles. We are too much accustomed to transfer to an earlier period associations which belong to a later one. If we read the Gospels by themselves, without interpolating facts drawn from the later books, we shall easily see that the twelve are there described as wholly unfit to be the supreme rulers of a church already organized; whereas after the descent of the Holy Spirit on the day of Pentecost, they appear as new men, clothed with every intellectual, spiritual, and miraculous endowment that was needed for the right administration of that kingdom which was now indeed set up externally, as well as in the hearts of all believers.

It is now for the first time that we begin to read of a "church," distinct from the old organization, and consisting of the apostles "and other disciples," to the number of one hundred and twenty, who had assembled together in an upper room until the day of Pentecost, when "there were added unto them about three thousand souls," who "continued steadfastly in the apostles' doctrine and fellowship, and in breaking of bread, and in prayers" (Acts 2 : 42). Here we have a society statedly assembling for prayer, praise, preaching, and communion, i. e. a church, and we accordingly find it stated in the same connection that "the Lord added to THE CHURCH daily such as should be saved" (Acts 2 : 47), and afterwards that "great fear came upon all THE CHURCH" (Acts 5 : 11), evidently meaning all the members of the body which had thus been gathered, and which is thenceforth usually called "the church" (e. g. Acts 8: 1, 3), until the establishment of other churches "throughout all Judea, Galilee, and Samaria" (Acts 9: 31), after which the original society is distinguished as "the church which was in Jerusalem" (Acts 8: 1. 11: 22), the more indefinite expression being thenceforth used to designate the whole Christian body, of which "the churches" were component parts or rather subdivisions (Acts 12: 1, 5), except in cases where the context evidently limits the application of the term to a local society or congregation. But with these distinctions the word *church* is, in the latter books, employed with a frequency which forms a striking contrast with the total silence of the four evangelists respecting any new organization.

We have seen that Christ came to establish a kingdom and re-organize the church. We may now add that this organization was to be essentially the same with that which had before existed. This is deducible from several obvious considerations. 1. As the Christian church was to be essentially identical with the Jewish, all that was permanent, even in the organization of the one, would of course be retained in the other. The kingly, priestly, and prophetical offices were thenceforth to be filled by Christ alone. The union of Church and State was to be done away by the extension of the church beyond the limits of a single nation. But the government of the people by elders, local and general, was wholly independent of these temporary institutions, and survived them all. It was therefore natural to expect, that it would be continued in the Christian church. 2. It was intrinsically suited to every variety of outward circumstances, in all ages, and all parts of the world. Being originally founded upon natural relations, and the family constitution, which is universal, it was well suited, by its simplicity, for general adoption, and by its efficiency, for the attainment of the ends proposed. 3. The intention to retain it was implied in our Lord's conduct with respect to the Jewish organization. He frequented the synagogues, or meetings of the people for public worship, in the towns or neighbourhoods where he chanced to be, and especially in the region where he was brought up. He complied with the usages of public worship, and exercised the privilege of expounding the Scriptures to the people. This respectful compliance with existing institutions he continued to the last; and his example was followed by his disciples. When they went abroad to preach, they availed themselves of the facilities afforded by existing institutions and arrangements. They always, if they could, preached in the synagogues. The first preaching, even to the heathen, was in synagogues. It was only where they found no synagogues, or when they were shut out from them, that they began to form separate societies. 4. When a separate organization did take place, it was on the ancient model. The first Christian church, as we have seen, was at Jerusalem. Now the organization of this "church that was in Jerusalem" is entitled to particular attention upon two accounts; first, because it was the mother church, from which the other churches were derived by propagation; then, because all the twelve apostles were, for a time, members of it. So far then as apostolical practice and example can be binding upon us, the history of this church must be highly instructive, in relation to the local constitution of the early Christian churches. Now at an early period, when a communication was made to the church at Jerusalem from one abroad, it was made to THE ELDERS (Acts 11: 30), and on a subsequent occasion to "the Apostles and Elders" (Acts 15: 2, 4, 6, 22), who united in passing a decree on an important question of faith and practice (Acts 16: 4). It seems, then, that even while the Apostles were in intimate connection with the church at Jerusalem, that church was governed by its Elders; and, what is particularly worthy of attention, we nowhere read of the original creation of this office in that church. We can trace the offices of Deacon and Apostle to their very origin, whereas that of Elder runs back far beyond the organization of the Christian church, and appears in the history as an arrangement, not springing out of a new state of things, but transferred from an old one.

Nor was this adoption of the eldership a mere fortuitous occurrence, much less a local peculiarity of the church in Jerusalem. It was extended, as a thing of course, to all affiliated churches. When Paul and Barnabas planted churches in Asia Minor, they ordained them Elders (Acts 14 : 23). Paul sent from Miletus for "the Elders of the Church" at Ephesus (Acts 20: 17). He directs Timothy how to treat Elders (1 Tim. 5: 1, 17, 19). He commands Titus to ordain Elders in every city of Crete (Titus 1: 5). James speaks of "the Elders of the Church" as of a body of men, which was not only well known to his readers, but which would exist of course in every Christian congregation (James 5: 14). Peter enjoins submission to the Elders, and classes himself among them (1 Peter

5: 1, 5). John calls himself an Elder in the title of his second and third epistle.

All this seems to show that the office of Elder was regarded as essential to the organization of a local or particular church. As to the mode of introducing it, we have no explicit information. The most probable hypothesis is one which I shall here state in the words of an eminent living dignitary of the Anglican Church. "It appears highly probable—I might say morally certain—that wherever a Jewish Synagogue existed that was brought, the whole or the chief part of it, to embrace the gospel, the Apostles did not there so much form a Christian church (or congregation, ecclesia), as make an existing congregation Christian, by introducing the Christian Sacraments and Worship, and establishing whatever regulations were necessary for the newly-adopted Faith; leaving the machinery (if I may so speak) of government unchanged; the rulers of synagogues, elders, and other officers (whether spiritual or ecclesiastical, or both) being already provided in the existing institutions. And it is likely that several of the earliest Christian churches did originate in this way, that is, that they were converted synagogues, which became Christian churches, as soon as the members, or the main part of the members, acknowledged Jesus as the Messiah. The attempt to effect this conversion of a Jewish synagogue into a Christian church, seems always to have been made, in the first instance, in every place where there was an opening for it. Even after the call of the idolatrous Gentiles, it appears plainly to have been the practice of the Apostles Paul and Barnabas, when they came to any city in which there was a synagogue, to go thither first and deliver their sacred message to the Jews and 'devout (or proselyte) Gentiles;' according to their own expression (Acts 13 : 16), to the 'men of Israel and those that feared God,' adding that it was necessary that the word of God should be 'first preached to them.' And when they found a church in any of those cities in which (and such was probably a very large majority) there was no Jewish synagogue that received the gospel, it is likely they would still conform, in a great measure, to the same model."*

In so doing, they would of course fix upon the natural elders, i. e. heads of families, as answering most nearly to the hereditary elders of the Jews. That the genealogical or patriarchal constitution was at once or by degrees disused, is not at all at variance with the supposition, that the Jewish eldership was transferred to the Christian Church, because one of the advantages of this organization is the ease with which it can adapt itself to any state of manners or condition of society, all that is really essential to it being the official preference of those who have a natural priority derived from age and family relations. Under the present constitution of society, as under that which was predominant in apostolic times throughout the Roman empire, the same ends, which were answered in the old theocracy by granting power to the chiefs of tribes and houses, are accomplished by intrusting it to those who sustain an analogous relation to society, that is, to men of mature age, and especially to actual heads of families. In either case the great end is accomplished of bringing the church under the same influence that

* The Kingdom of Christ Delineated. By Richard Whately, D.D., Archbishop of Dublin. pp. 84–86 (American edition).

rules the families of which it is composed. Whether all the heads of families were clothed with this authority, or only some selected for the purpose, is a question of detail, not at all affecting principle, and one which might perhaps admit of a solution varying with local and other unessential circumstances. One thing, however, appears certain, as an inference from all the facts which we have been considering, viz., that while some features of the Jewish polity were laid aside as temporary, the government by Elders was retained as a permanent principle of organization in the Christian Church. And here we meet with the only explanation of the fact already mentioned, that the creation of the office of Elder is nowhere recorded in the New Testament, as in the case of Deacons and Apostles, because the latter were created to meet new and special exigencies, while the former was transmitted from the earliest times. In other words, THE OFFICE OF ELDER WAS THE ONLY PERMANENT ESSENTIAL OFFICE OF THE CHURCH UNDER EITHER DISPENSATION.

ESSAY II.

ON THE POWERS OF THE PRIMITIVE PRESBYTERS.

THE conclusion reached in the preceding essay may be rendered still more certain by exhibiting direct proof of the fact, that presbyters, as presbyters, possessed and exercised the highest powers now belonging to the ministry, even in apostolic times, from which we may infer *a fortiori*, that the same authority is vested in them now.

It will be recollected, that the presbyterial office is coeval with the church, and that Paul and Barnabas, during their missionary tour in Asia Minor, not only planted churches, but "ordained them elders in every city." If then we can discover with what powers these early presbyters were clothed, we shall establish a sure basis for our subsequent inquiries. And in this investigation we are greatly aided by the preservation, in the Acts of the Apostles, of a valedictory address by Paul to certain persons of this class, when he was leaving Greece and Asia Minor for Jerusalem; in which address, we find not only strong expressions of his private feelings, and allusions to his ministerial labours, but advice to those whom he addressed, as to the right discharge of their official duties. It affords us, therefore, evidence, as to the functions of the primitive elders, which is none the less interesting or instructive, because furnished incidentally.

The statement here referred to is recorded in the twentieth chapter of Acts, where we read that "Paul had determined to sail by Ephesus, because he would not spend the time in Asia," "and from Miletus he sent to Ephesus, and called the elders of the church." When they were come, he appealed to them as witnesses of his fidelity to the churches of that region, in declaring unto them all the counsel of God. He then announces to them that his personal connection with them was dissolved for ever, and exhorts them to the diligent performance of the duties which would thenceforth be peculiarly incumbent on them. And in so doing, it is worthy of remark, that he makes no allusion to the intended substitution of another in his place, as their official guide and counsellor, but speaks to them precisely as he might, or rather must, have spoken, on the supposition, that from that time forth they were themselves to exercise the highest powers in the church of Ephesus. If he had still expected them to act as mere inferiors and assistants, he would naturally, not to say necessarily, have comforted their grief at his departure, by the promise of a competent successor, and in warning them of dangers by which their church was menaced, would of course have exhorted them to faithful and diligent co-operation with their bishop. But the passage contains nothing of all this; a circumstance which, though it may prove little by itself, as to the organization of the church at Ephesus, at least justifies the inference, that the powers here ascribed to the Ephesian presbyters were powers to be exercised in virtue of their presbyterial character, and not by delegation from a higher class of permanent church-officers. For if the apostle could direct them to perform these acts, not only without making his own presence and concurrence a prerequisite, but in such terms as really exclude it, how much less reason have we to believe, that their validity was meant to be dependent on the sanction of a bishop, who is not so much as mentioned, and of whose existence we have no proof elsewhere?

Nor is this a mere negative deduction from Paul's silence, as to any superior authority at Ephesus; for the same thing is implied in the choice of his expressions. "Take heed, therefore, unto yourselves,"—*therefore,* since you are now to be deprived of the extraordinary temporary supervision which you have enjoyed, and to be left with the whole burden of the church upon you; under this change of circumstances you must be watchful on your own account, not only for your personal safety and advantage, but for that of the church also—"take heed, therefore, unto yourselves, and to all the flock," not the flock of another shepherd, but their own, for which they were directly responsible—"over the which the Holy Ghost hath made you overseers," ἐπισκόπους or bishops. The bearing of this usage of the term upon the general question of episcopal organization need not be discussed in this place. All that it is necessary here to notice is, that these Ephesian presbyters were shepherds of God's flock, not described as under-shepherds, that is, as the deputies of any human shepherd, but as constituted such by God himself, and that not merely by his providential dispensations, but by a special designation of the Holy Ghost. This explicit mention of the *jus divinum* under which they acted, when viewed in connection with the absence of all reference to any higher local power, either actual or prospective, makes it not only improbable, but scarcely possible, that what they are empowered or required to do, was to be done by delegation, or in any other way than by direct authority from God himself, bestowed upon them as the highest permanent and local rulers of the church of Ephesus.

With these views of the character in which the elders are addressed, and of the right by which their functions were to be discharged, let us now endeavour to determine, in the same way, what these functions were. The answer to this question is afforded by the words immediately succeeding those already quoted. "Take heed, therefore, unto yourselves, and to all the flock, over the which the Holy Ghost hath made you overseers, TO FEED THE CHURCH OF GOD, which he hath purchased with his own blood." As the church has been already represented as a flock, the official duty of these elders towards it is described by a cognate metaphor. The exact correspondence of the terms is less apparent in our version than in the original, where the word rendered *flock*, and that rendered *to feed*, are collateral derivatives from a common root, and stand in the same relation to the word which means *a shepherd.* To the verb, both etymology and usage give the sense, not of *feeding* merely, but of *acting as a shepherd, doing a shepherd's duty,* of which feeding is a most essential part, but not by any means the whole, since it would either be impossible or unavailing, without further care in guiding to the fold and to the pasture, in collecting and reclaiming, in protecting from the weather and from beasts of prey, and in other slight but indispensable attentions, all included in the literal vocation of a shepherd, and in both the literal and the figurative import of the Greek verb which Paul uses. Unless then the English verb *to feed* be taken with such latitude of meaning as to comprehend all this, it no more expresses the whole duty of a shepherd (as the Greek word does), than the verb *to shoot* describes the business of a soldier or a hunter, or *to plough* that of a farmer. It is highly important that our exposition of this passage should be wholly unaffected by a prejudice, connected only with the English version, and arising from its failure to express the full sense of Paul's phraseology. Even when figuratively used, the verb *ποιμαίνω* is employed by the Greek writers to denote not merely *nourishment* but *care*, in the most extensive sense of the expression, such care as faithful shepherds give to helpless and dependent flocks. If then the church at Ephesus was a spiritual flock, and these its elders were spiritual shepherds, the duty here enjoined upon them is not merely that of feeding them with knowledge, by public and private teaching, but also that of governing, controlling, and protecting them, as well from the effects of internal corruption, as from those of violence and fraud *ab extra*. It is, in short, a metaphorical description of the ministerial office, in its whole extent, as comprehending all that is essential to the continued existence of the church, and the attainment of the ends for which it was established, just as the business of a shepherd comprehends all that is necessary to the safety and well-being of the flock. There is no more reason in the text itself, for excluding any of the ministerial functions from the figurative import of the verb *ποιμαίνειν*, than there is for excluding some things in the nature and condition of the church from the figurative import of the substantive *ποίμνιον*; if the latter is a general description of the church, the former is a general description of the ministry, its duties and its powers. And this, which is the natural and obvious meaning of the figurative terms which the apostle uses, agrees, in all points, with his subsequent expressions. "For I know this, that after my departing shall grievous wolves"—a common figure for false teachers—"enter in among you, not sparing the flock. Also of your own selves shall men arise, speaking perverse things, to draw away disciples after them." These are the two great evils, with which the church was threatened, error of doctrine, and schism as the consequence; for this is the relative position of the two things, as described in Scripture, not the converse, as maintained by those who make purity of doctrine to depend upon external regularity, as we shall see hereafter. To prevent these evils, whether threatened from within or from without, and to prevent them, not by private effort merely, but by authoritative action, is distinctly made the duty of the presbyters of Ephesus.

That the apostle refers not to personal but official influence, appears from the solemn mention of their designation by the Holy Ghost, with which he prefaces his exhortation. There would be something quite incongruous in making the divine right of these presbyters the ground of an injunction which was equally binding upon all true Christians. This would be tantamount to saying, since the Holy Ghost has placed you in high official station, be assiduous in personal and private duties. If, on the other hand, the reference is clearly to the influence exerted by these presbyters, as such, and in the exercise of their distinctive functions, then the question meets us, How could they comply with this injunction, unless they were intrusted with the keys both of discipline and doctrine, with the power, not of teaching merely, but of maintaining purity of doctrine, by deciding controversies, trying heretics, silencing false teachers, and excluding from the ministry all such as were esteemed by them unfaithful or unfit? But these are acts supposing the possession of the highest powers now belonging to the ministry, not merely those of preaching and of ordinary pastoral control, but also those of ministerial discipline and ordination.

It may be objected, that the duty, to which the elders, in the next verse, are specifically called, is not that of judging or of acting with authority, but merely that of watching and remembering his former admonitions, and that this implies the existence of a higher power, which alone was competent to check the evil. But if this be so, how is it that he does not even mention or allude to such superior power? It cannot be imagined, that he merely meant to terrify the elders by predicting future evils to the church, without suggesting a preventive or a remedy; and yet this is undoubtedly the case, if those whom he addresses could do nothing more than watch and bear in mind his warnings. If it be said, that the elders must have been aware of the existence of these "higher powers," and needed not to be informed of it by Paul, it then becomes impossible to understand why he addressed his exhortations to the presbyters, and not to their superiors, who alone had power to prevent or remedy the threatened evil. Nor can this difficulty be removed by taking it for granted, first, that there was a bishopric of Ephesus, above the eldership, and then that it was vacant, so that Paul was under the necessity, at this time, of addressing the "inferior clergy." For in that case he could hardly have omitted all allusion to the fact assumed, and all injunction to obey the bishop, when he should be sent, and co-operate with him for the prevention of the evils to be feared; whereas, he seems, as we have seen, to throw the whole responsibility upon the elders, and addresses them precisely as he must have done, if he expected and intended the entire care of the Ephesian church to be devolved on them. To take the contrary for granted, in despite of the obvious tenor of Paul's language, is, in effect, to destroy the value of all proof derived from language, except in the case of an explicit, categorical assertion, which is granted, upon all sides, to be wanting here. A simple test of probability, in this case, is afforded by the fact, that no one, reading the apostle's exhortation, either could or would derive from it the notion of an ecclesiastical authority at Ephesus, above that of the presbyters, to whom the exhortation is addressed; and on the other hand, that no one so reading it, could fail to gather from it, in itself considered, that these elders were invested with official right and power to prevent or to redress the evils here predicted.

The truth is, that the other supposition rests upon the foregone conclusion, that a prelatical authority, distinct from the presbyterate, did certainly exist at Ephesus, and that the subjection of the elders to it is implied or presupposed in the apostle's exhortation. But, those who deny that any proof of such authority exists in any quarter, and interpret Paul's language by itself and by the context, without reference to any preconceived hypothesis whatever, will be forced to the conclusion, that he here addresses the Ephesian elders as the rulers of the church, and that when he exhorts them to be watchful and remember, he refers not to private but official vigilance, and to such a recollection of his warnings as would lead to the due exercise of their authority in quenching the insidious fires of heresy and schism, which they could not do without possessing all the power which a bishop, or derivative apostle, on the opposite hypothesis, could possibly have exercised. The objection to the argument from this address of Paul, that it does not ascribe to the Ephesian elders the specific powers of discipline and ordination, proves too much; for it would prove that they were not even authorized to preach or to administer the sacraments, since these are not specifically mentioned, though included in the figurative meaning of *ποιμαίνειν*, which, however, includes more, and is descriptive of the ministerial work in general, as we have seen already. The apostle speaks of them, either as having all the ministerial powers, or as having none; because the terms which he employs are those of general description, not minute specification, and must either be descriptive of the office as a whole, or not at all.

But even granting, for the sake of argument, that *ποιμαίνειν* merely means *to feed*, and that feeding is a metaphor for preaching and the sacraments, it does not follow, that the powers of discipline and ordination, although not specifically mentioned, are excluded. It is clear, not only that the whole includes its parts, but also that the greater may include the less. As the general ascription of the ministerial powers to these elders would imply that they possessed each separately, so too the ascription of a higher ministerial power might imply that they possessed a lower. Now discipline and ordination, it will be admitted, derive their value from the ends which they promote, and which they were intended to secure. The end of discipline is to preserve purity, and to exclude the unworthy from the privileges of the church. The end of ordination is to secure a valid ministration of the word and sacraments. But the word and the sacraments themselves have an independent and intrinsic value. If the power of dispensing them had been conferred on any who thought proper to make use of it, without any special ordination to an office, whatever inconveniences might have attended that arrangement, it could not have impaired the intrinsic value of the word and sacraments. But if, on the other hand, there were no word or sacraments, ordination would be useless. And the same may be said, mutatis mutandis, as to government or discipline. These then, to wit, ordination and discipline, are subsidiary functions, which derive their value from the relation they sustain to others. The possession of these powers, therefore, might have been inferred from the possession of the higher powers upon which they are dependent, even if the latter had alone been mentioned. But the fact, as we have seen already, is, that all the powers of the ministry collectively are comprehended in the metaphor of acting as a shepherd to the flock of Christ.

If it should be alleged in this case, as it has been in some others, that the powers, apparently ascribed to presbyters, were really intended to be exercised by bishops, here included under the generic name of elders, it may be replied, that such a mode of reasoning precludes the possibility of proving any thing, except so far as the opposing party may think proper to allow it. If the ascription of a certain power to a certain class of officers, distinctly named, is not a proof of their possessing it, the fact is not susceptible of proof at all. And this extraordinary process, let it be observed, is equally available on either side of a disputed question. If one man may explain away the acts ascribed to presbyters as the exclusive acts of bishops, then another may explain away the acts ascribed to deacons as the exclusive acts of presbyters. It should also be observed, that if one of the official acts ascribed to presbyters may be explained away as the exclusive act of a superior order, any other of the acts so ascribed may be explained in the same manner. If, when presbyters are spoken of as exercising all the ministerial powers, one may argue that bishops are the only elders who are thus empowered to ordain, another may, with equal right, allege that bishops are the only elders authorized to preach or to baptize, and that the primitive presbyters did neither, by themselves or in their own right, but merely united, as assessors, in the preaching and baptizing acts of their superiors in office. To an argument which naturally leads to such results, it is sufficient to oppose a simple negative, by saying that as bishops or apostles are not mentioned in the text, the official acts ascribed to presbyters were meant to be considered as performed by them alone in that capacity. When therefore Paul describes the presbyters of Ephesus as having been divinely called to act as shepherds of God's flock, we must regard it as a proof that all the powers of the ministry, including those of discipline and ordination, were possessed and exercised by elders, even in the days of the apostles.

A large part of what has now been said applies, with equal force, to 1 Tim. 5 : 17, where the same apostle speaks, on a different occasion, not only of the same office, but of the same men, not only of elders in general, but of Ephesian elders in particular. Assuming that *πρεσβύτεροι* is here a name of office, it cannot be descriptive of the office of apostle or apostle-bishop, partly for the reason above given in another case, that the assumption is entirely gratuitous, partly because Timothy, according to the adverse theory, would then be represented as a hyper-apostolical church-officer, not only equal but superior to Paul, who was merely an apostle. If, on the other hand, the word denotes presbyters or elders, in the proper sense, then the apostle must be speaking of the powers which belonged to them in that capacity, and not as the mere agents of a higher power. That no superiority of Timothy to these Ephesian elders is implied in the apostle's words, will be proved in another place, and may be here assumed.

Since then it is of elders that he speaks, and of elders acting in their own right, we have only to inquire what official functions are ascribed to them, in order to determine what were the powers of a presbyter or elder in apostolic times. "Let the EL-

DERS THAT RULE well be counted worthy of double honour." They are here distinctly recognized as rulers in the church, and this must surely comprehend the right of discipline, if not of ordination. It may be said, however, that *προεστῶτες* merely means presiding, holding the first place in the society, and therefore denotes relative position, but not office or official power. It will scarcely be disputed, however, that *πρεσβύτεροι* denotes official rank; and whether *προεστῶτες* does not signify the exercise of an official power, is a question which can only be determined by a reference to usage. In Rom. 12: 8, *ὁ προϊστάμενος* cannot denote mere priority of rank or conspicuous position, for two reasons: first, because a man could not be exhorted to hold such a position with diligence; and secondly, because all the other terms connected with it signify specific actions. The same thing is evident from the collocation of *προϊσταμένους* in 1 Thess. 5: 12, between *κοπιῶντας* and *νουθετοῦντας*, both denoting specific functions of the ministry. In 1 Tim. 3: 4, the bishop is described as one that ruleth well (*καλῶς προϊστάμενον*) his own house, which can hardly mean one who holds the first place in it, without any original jurisdiction over it. Let the sense which *προΐστημι* evidently has in all these cases, be applied to that before us, and it follows of course, that presbyters or bishops are here spoken of as ruling the church, just as really as they are elsewhere said to rule their families. That the government referred to is that of the church, appears from what follows in the same verse, as to labouring in word and doctrine. If, then, *πρεσβύτεροι* is here a name of office, which will scarcely be denied by those, who use this text to prove Timothy's superiority to presbyters, then the officers described by it are clearly recognized as rulers in the church, without any reference whatever to a superior human power. Where shall we find an equally distinct ascription of the ruling power to apostles, not of the original thirteen?

Here then are two passages, in which the same apostle speaks of the Ephesian elders, first metaphorically as the shepherds of Christ's flock, then literally as the rulers of the church. Whatever doubt might be supposed to rest upon the meaning of the terms employed, in either case, may be disposed of by comparing them together. That ποιμαίνειν does not merely denote *feeding*, whether literal or spiritual, but the whole extent of the pastoral care, including government, may now be argued from the προεστῶτες of the parallel passage. And that προεστῶτες, on the other hand, includes the powers of discipline and ordination, is rendered still more probable by Paul's exhorting these same elders, in the other case, to duties which imply the possession of these powers. The two texts, taken in conjunction, so as to explain each other, warrant us in stating as a general fact, that the Ephesian elders are twice spoken of by Paul as rulers of the church, without any intimation that the power of ordination is to be excepted, or that they acted in subjection to a bishop.

Now the terms of this description must be applicable, either to presbyters in general, or to the presbyters of Ephesus exclusively. The latter supposition would imply, that there was no uniformity in primitive church-government, the same class of officers possessing different powers in different cases, an hypothesis destructive of all arguments against presbyterian orders, founded on alleged deviations from the apostolic model. We have moreover a direct proof that this organization was a general one in the first epistle of Peter, where he addresses the elders, not of one church merely, but of Pontus, Galatia, Cappadocia, Asia, and Bithynia; calls himself their fellow-elder, and exhorts them to "feed the flock of God"—the same expression used by Paul to the Ephesian elders—"taking the oversight thereof, not by constraint but willingly, not for filthy lucre, but of a ready mind; neither as being lords over God's heritage,"—implying that they were under a temptation so to do, which could scarcely be the case, if they were mere assessors to a bishop—"and when the chief shepherd shall appear"—this clearly implies that they were under-shepherds only to the head of the church—"ye shall receive a crown of glory that fadeth not away." If it can be supposed that all the churches of Pontus, Galatia, Cappadocia, Asia, and Bithynia, were accidentally deprived of bishops at this time, it would go far to prove that the privation was a matter of but little moment. If, however, this description has respect to presbyters in general, we have proof that the primitive presbyters were rulers of the church, and no proof that discipline and ordination were excepted from their powers.

With the general view, which we have thus obtained from Scripture, of the presbyterial office as a whole, let us now compare the more specific language of the apostle Paul to Timothy: "Neglect not the gift that is in thee, which was given thee by prophecy, with the laying on of the hands of the presbytery" (1 Tim. 4: 14). If this does not relate to ordination, there can be no reason for supposing that the parallel passage in 2 Tim. 1: 6 relates to ordination; and as the transaction recorded in Acts 13: 1–3 was nothing more than a solemn designation to a special service, the result is, that we have in the New Testament no proof that any rite of ordination was considered necessary, nor any instance of its having been performed, the word sometimes rendered by the English verb "ordain" being a general expression for the act of constituting or appointing. So far, then, from the act of ordination, as distinct from that of designation or appointment, being formally reserved, as the peculiar prerogative of a superior order in the ministry, it does not seem to have been used at all, and the general terms in which the presbyters are spoken of, as rulers of the church, are to be understood as comprehending all the powers necessary to its maintenance and government. But even granting that the text relates to ordination in the proper sense, it has been alleged that the ordaining act is not ascribed to presbyters, as such, but to apostles. In support of this assertion, very different positions have been taken. In the first place it has been alleged, that the presbytery may have consisted wholly of apostles. Not to reiterate the reasons which have been already given, for resisting all gratuitous assumptions, tending to reverse the natural import of language, and to render proof impossible, we answer this objection by a counter allegation, that the presbytery may have consisted wholly of mere presbyters. The two possibilities will balance one another, and in choosing between them, the word *πρεσβυτέριον* must have due weight. It is certainly more likely, in the absence of explicit proof, that *πρεσβυτέριον*, if it means a body of men at all, means a body of mere presbyters, than that it means a body of apostles. The apostles, being presbyters, might be included in the name; but as they had a distinctive title of their own, it is natural to suppose, that if their distinctive functions were the subject of discourse, their distinctive title would be used, and, on the other hand, that when the generic title is employed, the functions spoken of are not the peculiar functions of apostles, as apostles, but those which are common to them and presbyters. Or even if πρεσβυτέριον here denotes apostles, the use of the name in this connection shows that it was in the character of presbyters that they ordained. It seems incredible that if they held two offices, a higher and a lower, those acts which they performed by virtue of the former should be connected with the title of the latter. The bishops of the Protestant Episcopal Church are in some cases rectors of particular parishes. When we read, therefore, of a man as rector of a certain church, we may be reading of a bishop; but no one acquainted with the true facts of the case would speak of a bishop by the other title, when ascribing to him acts which, according to the customs of that church, could only be performed by him as bishop. On the other hand, the official record of a baptism, as having been administered by the rector of a church, would be regarded as conclusive evidence that parochial clergymen have power to baptize; nor would it be invalidated by the allegation, that as the rector in question was a bishop, it was in the latter character alone that he baptized; much less by the suggestion that he *may* have been a bishop, and that ordinary rectors therefore had no such authority. If, then, the apostles are here mentioned as ordainers, and as forming a *πρεσβυτέριον* for the purpose, it must have been in the character of presbyters that they ordained. Supposing, then, that *πρεσβυτέριον* means a body of men, it matters not of whom it was composed; for, whatever else they may have been, they must have been presbyters, and as such they ordained.

To escape from this dilemma, it has been alleged, that *πρεσβυτέριον* denotes, not the ordainers, but the office of a presbyter. To this there are two very serious objections. In the first place, the construction is unusual and unnatural, the laying on of the hands of an office. According to all usage and analogy, the genitive after *χειρῶν* must denote the persons to whom the hands belonged, and by whom the imposition was performed. Can it be fortuitous that, out of more than a hundred other cases, in which some form of *χείρ* is followed in construction by the genitive, there is not one in which it can be supposed to signify any thing except the person whose hands are mentioned? Or can it be supposed, that the relation of *τοῦ πρεσβυτερίου* to *χειρῶν*, in the case before us, is different from that of *μου* to the same word, in the precisely parallel expression, 2 Tim. 1 : 6? The other objection to this interpretation of the word is, that in the only other places where it occurs in the New Testament (Luke 22 : 66. Acts 22 : 5), it means, and can mean, nothing but a body of *πρεσβύτεροι*. Before we can explain it of the office, therefore, we must adopt, first, an unnatural and unparalleled construction, and then, an unauthorized meaning of the principal word. That is to say, it cannot be so explained without doing violence both to lexicography and grammar.

But there is still another method of evading the conclusion, that presbyters are here represented as ordaining. This is by asserting, that even if πρεσβυτέριον does mean a body of elders, μετά does not mean *by* but *with*, denoting mere participation, not authoritative action, so that presbyters are not represented as ordaining, but merely as joining in the ordination. This view of the passage takes for granted, first, that the preposition cannot mean *by*, but must mean *with;* and then, that if it does mean *with*, it must connect the action of the presbyters, as mere assessors, with the authoritative act of the apostles, as ordainers. Both these assumptions are entirely unauthorized. The Greek μετά, like the English *with*, has sometimes the secondary sense of *by*, *by means of.* The origin of this secondary meaning seems to be, that the agent acts *with* his instrument, in the strict sense, i. e. in company with it; and thus the preposition, which strictly conveys this idea only, conveys by implication that of instrumentality. The transition from the one sense to the other may be seen in such expressions as the following: "Pursue him with the sword, and then destroy him with the sword." In the first phrase, *with* denotes merely that the sword is to accompany the pursuers; in the second it denotes, that the sword is the instrument, by which they are to act. This etymological analysis is confirmed by the usage of the New Testament. "Thou shalt make me full of joy with (μετά) thy countenance" (Acts 2 : 28). This cannot mean 'thou, together with thy countenance, shalt make me full of joy'—nor, 'thou shalt make me, together with thy countenance, full of joy'—but 'thou, by means of thy countenance (or presence), shalt make me full of joy.' The same thing, in substance, may be said of Acts 13: 17, "and *with* an high arm brought he them out of it." In Acts 14: 27 we read, that when Paul and Barnabas returned to Antioch, "they gathered the church together and rehearsed all that God had done with them (*μετ' αὐτῶν*)," and again, Acts 15: 4, "they declared all things that God had done with them." This does not mean "to them," as it might possibly in English, because even if *μετά* is used elsewhere in that sense, the context here shows that the historian means what God had done to the Gentiles *by* them or *through* them, as his instruments. These examples will suffice to show, that *μετὰ* may mean *by*, as well as *with*, and that it is not, therefore, to be taken for granted, that it here expresses a different kind of action.

Granting, however, that it does mean *with*, in the strict sense, what two things does it connect? The imposition of hands with what? The adverse argument assumes, not only that it may, but that it must, connect the imposition of hands by the presbytery with the ordaining act of the apostle, which is not mentioned at all. Now if any rule of construction can be looked upon as fixed, it is, that what is expressed, other things being equal, must be preferred to what is not expressed but merely conjectured or supposed. According to this principle, *μετά*, if it merely means *together with*, must connect the imposition of the hands of the presbytery with the prophecy or revelation, mentioned just before. How was the gift conferred on Timothy? By means of a divine communication, *διὰ προφητείας*. By that alone? No, but by that, *together with* the laying on of hands, which is essentially equivalent to saying, 'by revelation *and* the imposition of hands.' Whatever force the διά has in relation to προφητείας it has in relation to ἐπιθέσεως, the μετά serving merely to connect them.

We are then reduced to this alternative. If μετά is a mere connective, it connects προφητείας with ἐπιθέσεως, and implies that the ordination was as much effected by the one as by the other, or that both were alike instruments or channels of communication, by which the gift of God was conveyed to Timothy. But if μετά is more than a connective, and itself denotes *by means of*, then the act of the presbytery is itself described as the medium or instrument of ordination. On the whole, then, it appears, that unless we give to πρεσβυτέριον a meaning which it has not elsewhere, and connect it with the words before it in a manner which is utterly at variance with the usage of the language, or assume, without necessity or right, that it here denotes a body of apostles, or that the action of apostles, although not expressed, is understood, and that of the presbytery made dependent on it, we are under the necessity of drawing the conclusion, that presbyters, in apostolic times, ordained. And this, which is the only exposition of the text that harmonizes fully with the usage of the words and with the principles of grammar, that supposes nothing and imagines nothing, but allows the text to speak for itself, is moreover recommended by its perfect agreement with the natural and obvious meaning of the passages before considered, in which presbyters are spoken of as bearing the whole burden of church government, and called to duties which imply the power not only of discipline but of ordination.

But although these passages contain enough to warrant the conclusion, that the primitive presbyters possessed and exercised the highest powers now belonging to the ministry, it cannot be denied, that this conclusion would be rendered more completely satisfying, if it were possible to cite a case, in which there could be no dispute or doubt, in relation either to the acts described, or to the persons represented as performing them, on both which points there is some room for diversity of judgment in the cases just considered, though the balance of probabilities appears to be decidedly in favour of the ground already stated. But this preponderance would be rendered more decided and conspicuous by the collateral evidence even of a single case, in which all parties could agree that certain persons are described as exercising certain powers. Now there happens to be not only one case of the kind supposed, but two, which require to be distinctly stated.

It is granted, upon all sides, that Timothy in Ephesus, and Titus in Crete, possessed and exercised the highest powers now belonging to the ministry. So fully is this fact admitted by most Episcopal writers, that they build upon it their most specious argument, to prove that the apostolic office is perpetual. The objections to that argument have been already stated; but the fact upon which it is founded, we agree with our opponents in asserting. We maintain, with them, that there are no ministerial functions now existing in the church, which were not exercised by Timothy and Titus, who are clearly recognized as having power, not only to preach and administer the sacraments but to dain and govern. It is, however, a matter of some moment to observe the nature of the evidence, which forms the ground of this unanimous conclusion. The point at which we differ is the question whether the possession of these powers necessarily supposes a superiority of permanent official rank in Timothy and Titus above presbyters. The reasons for believing that it does not, have already been detailed, and what is now designed is merely to direct attention to the nature of the evidence, by which the opposite opinion is sustained, and which is certainly not destitute of plausibility. The argument may be succinctly stated thus, that since the right of ordination and of ministerial discipline is recognized by Paul, in his epistles to these two men, as belonging to them, they must of necessity have been superior to the presbyters whom they were to ordain and discipline.

This conclusion is vitiated by the false assumption, upon which it rests, that ordination to an office in the church can only be derived from one who holds a higher office, and that ministers of equal rank cannot mutually discipline each other. But for this defect, the reasoning would be conclusive. They are clearly commanded to ordain and exercise authority, and this, if inconsistent with equality of rank and identity of office, would demonstrate their superiority to presbyters. It will not, however, be contended, even by the warmest advocates of this opinion, that the evidence of this superiority, contained in Paul's epistles, is the strongest that can be imagined. They will grant, not only that a formal categorical assertion of the fact disputed would be stronger proof than that which is derived by inference from Paul's instructions, but that even in default of such assertion, the contested point might possibly have been much more indisputable than it is. If, for example, it had been recorded, as a historical fact, that Timothy and Titus acted towards the presbyters of Ephesus and Crete as their official inferiors, directing their movements and controlling the discharge of their official duties by minute instructions, the proof of their superiority would no doubt be regarded by our opponents as stronger than it now is. And the evidence would surely be considered as still more decisive, if among the books of the New Testament there were epistles written by Timothy and Titus to the presbyters of Ephesus and Crete; containing no recognition of equality, beyond what is habitually used by modern bishops to their youngest clergy; directing the movements of the elders in a positive and peremptory manner, without any reference to their own inclination or opinion; the superior rank of the two writers would be looked upon as quite indisputable. But if, in addition to all this, the elders were required to exercise their highest powers as the representatives or delegates of Timothy and Titus, with directions to pursue a certain course, until the writers should be personally present, and with kind but authoritative hints as to the personal improvement of the presbyters addressed; it must be owned that the denial of superior official rank in Timothy and Titus would be hopeless.

Now it happens, unfortunately for the adverse argument, that no such evidence exists, in reference to Timothy and Titus, whose superiority to presbyters must stand or fall with the assumption, that the power of ordination and of discipline implies a permanent diversity of rank. But what especially deserves attention is the interesting fact, that the very evidence, which would be universally acknowledged as sufficient to establish the superiority of Timothy and Titus with respect to presbyters, does certainly exist in the case of Paul with respect to Timothy and Titus themselves. The facts which constitute this evidence have been already stated in detail, but in different connections. That their bearing on the question now before us may be seen, a brief recapitulation will be necessary, under several particulars.

And first, let it be observed, that in the other books of the New Testament, that is to say, excepting the three epistles to Timothy and Titus, they are mentioned in a manner, which not only furnishes no proof of their equality to Paul, but naturally leads to the conclusion of their being his inferiors in rank and office. In the Acts of the Apostles, it will not be disputed, that Timothy appears as Paul's inferior, a young man chosen to attend him in his missionary travels, as a helper and a confidential messenger. It may be said, indeed, that it would not be fair to argue, from the first stage of Timothy's career, that he was always Paul's inferior; and this is true. But if we find Paul subsequently speaking of and to him, in a tone precisely suited to this original relation of the parties, it will surely make it highly probable, to say the least, that this relation still continued to subsist. And that this is really the case will be perceived upon comparing the place occupied by Timothy, as Paul's personal attendant, in the Acts of the Apostles (16 : 2. 17 : 15. 18 : 5. 19 : 22. 20 : 4), with the way in which Paul speaks to the Corinthians of having sent Timotheus to them, and requests that he may be among them without fear, and that no man may despise him, and that he may be sent back to the

Apostle in due time (1 Cor. 16 : 10, 11). It is plain from these words, not only that Timothy was acting as Paul's messenger and under his direction, but also that the service was a temporary one, and that when it was accomplished, he was to return to his accustomed duties, as the apostle's personal attendant. And that this was not a solitary case of such employment, is apparent from the first epistle to the Thessalonians, where Paul speaks first of having sent Timotheus to them (ch. 3 : 2), and then of his return and of the news which he brought back (v. 6); to which may be added Phil. 2 : 19, where he intimates his purpose to send Timotheus to them, not to remain there, but to bring him an account of their condition. In this last case, the execution of the purpose is left dependent upon Paul's own movements and convenience (v. 23), with an intimation that the sending of Timothy was merely meant to be a substitute for the apostle's personal attendance (v. 24). The relation between Timothy and Paul, apparent in these passages, may be compared to that between an aid-de-camp and his commander, the two main duties, in both cases, being those of personal attendance and of active service in communicating orders.

That the relative position of Titus was the same, may be inferred from Paul's allusion to "the coming of Titus," as of one who had been absent upon special duty, to the report which he had made of the state of things at Corinth, and to the effect produced upon him by his visit to the church there (2 Cor. 7 : 6, 7, 13, 15). It may also be observed that the Apostle speaks of the obedience and respect with which the Corinthians had treated Titus, as a mark of their submission to his own apostolical authority (vs. 15, 16).

Another incidental reference to Paul's employing Titus in this manner may be found in 2 Tim. 4 : 10, where he is mentioned among Paul's immediate followers. "Demas hath forsaken me, having loved this present world, and is departed unto Thessalonica; Crescens to Galatia; Titus to Dalmatia; only Luke is with me; take Mark and bring him with thee; for he is profitable to me εἰς διακονίαν," not "for the ministry" in general, but as a διάκονος or personal assistant in my labours. It seems plain that all the persons here named bore the same relation to the apostle, and were equally under his authority. Although Titus, therefore, is not mentioned in the Acts, there can be no doubt that his course began, like Timothy's, in personal attendance upon Paul in his journeys, to which indeed we find express allusion in Gal. 2 : 1, 3, where his Greek descent and circumcision are referred to, and the fact recorded of his having gone with Paul and Barnabas, on a particular occasion, to Jerusalem.

Both from the history and the epistles, therefore, independently of those addressed to Timothy and Titus, it would naturally be inferred, that these men were inferior to Paul, and acted under his direction. It may, indeed, be said, that they are clearly recognized as ministers; that Timothy is mentioned as Paul's workfellow (Rom. 16: 21), "one that worketh the work of the Lord even as I do" (1 Cor. 16: 10), as a "brother" (2 Cor. 1: 1), who had "served" with Paul "in the gospel" (Phil. 2: 22); that Titus likewise is described as his "brother" (2 Cor. 2: 13), his "partner and fellow-labourer" with respect to the Corinthians (2 Cor. 8: 23). All this is very true, and proves conclusively that Timothy and Titus were duly ordained ministers, and as such held the rank of presbyters or elders. But this, so far from proving their equality to Paul, strengthens the proof of their inferiority, by bringing their acknowledged ministerial standing into contrast with the manifest assumption of superiority on Paul's part. His continuing to regulate their movements after their admission to the ministry, shows clearly that he was superior, not only as a minister to private Christians, but as an apostle to mere presbyters or elders.

If it should be alleged, however, that Timothy and Titus were themselves invested with this same superiority, and that it is in this capacity that Paul addresses them, this is a question which can only be determined by an examination of the three epistles. If it be true that Paul's superiority to Timothy and Titus ceased before the date of his epistles to them, we may certainly expect to find the tone of his address to them materially altered, and the habit of express command exchanged for that of brotherly suggestion. And we do indeed find many strong expressions of fraternal or rather of paternal love, but mingled with peremptory and direct commands, as well as incidental intimations of superior authority upon the writer's part, some of which might be considered dubious or of little moment, if we did not know the mutual relation of the parties at an earlier date. The hypothesis that Timothy had now attained equality of rank with Paul, though not contradicted, is certainly not favoured by those parts of these epistles, in which Paul speaks of having left him at Ephesus for a special purpose (1 Tim. 1: 3) and renews the commission under which he acted (v. 18), gives him particular directions for his conduct until he shall come (ch. 3: 14, 15. 4: 13, 14), and summons Timothy to come within a certain time (2 Tim. 4: 21) and take the place of those who had just left him (ch. 4: 9–12), bringing Paul's cloak and parchments with him (v. 13).

Titus also is described as being left in Crete by Paul, to finish that which he had left undone (Tit. 1: 5), and is required to rejoin him, when relieved by Artemas or Tychicus (Tit. 3: 12). All this goes to prove that no such change had taken place in the relations of these men to Paul as would make them no longer his inferiors in office. And the same thing, though it could not be directly proved, is certainly corroborated by the numerous advices which he gives them with a view to their personal improvement; as when he exhorts Timothy to hold faith and a good conscience (1 Tim. 1: 19), to refuse profane and old wives' fables and exercise himself unto godliness (1 Tim. 4: 7), to give attendance to reading, exhortation and doctrine (v. 13), to let his proficiency appear to all (v. 15), to take heed to himself and to the doctrine that he may be saved (v. 16), to avoid covetousness and follow after righteousness, godliness, faith, love, patience, meekness (ch. 6: 11), to fight the good fight of faith and lay hold on eternal life (v. 12), to keep Paul's commandment without spot, unrebukable, until the appearing of our Lord Jesus Christ (v. 14), to avoid profane and vain babblings and oppositions of science falsely so called (1 Tim. 6: 20. 2 Tim. 2: 16), to be strong in the grace that is in Christ Jesus (2 Tim. 2: 1), to endure hardness as a good soldier of Jesus Christ (v. 3), to avoid foolish and unlearned questions (v. 23), to flee youthful lusts and follow righteousness, faith, charity, and peace (v. 22), to continue in the things which he had learned of Paul (2 Tim. 3: 14), and to endure afflictions (2 Tim. 4: 5).

It may be said, that all these are expressions, which might naturally be used by a man of Paul's celebrity and standing in the church, even to those holding the same office, if much younger than himself, and still more if they were his spiritual children. Admitting this to be a sufficient explanation of the general tone of Paul's epistles, and of his exhortations to mere personal and private duties, will it answer the same purpose, with respect to his authoritative directions for the exercise of their official functions? Can it be supposed that such minute instructions, as to public worship, ordination, discipline, and the duties to be enjoined upon different classes of society, would have been given to any but inferiors in rank and office? Such a hypothesis might be admissible, if every thing else in the epistles favoured it; but not when their whole drift and tenor make it scarcely possible to doubt that Timothy and Titus are addressed as Paul's inferiors. There are several classes of objections to the opposite opinion, every one of which would seem decisive unless countervailed by other circumstances. The general tone of the epistles is almost enough to show that Paul was their superior in office. It would fail to do so, if there were express recognitions of equality; but there are none. His dictation to them, with respect to the discharge of their official functions, would be almost enough to prove the point. Above all, the distinct allusions to their acting merely as Paul's messengers and delegates, without renouncing their relation to him as his personal attendants, make it almost certain. Now as each of these distinctive features of the three epistles is almost sufficient of itself to prove what is alleged, and as none of them detracts from any of the others, it may be safely stated as the most probable conclusion from the data generally, that the men, to whom these three epistles were addressed, were no less subject to Paul's authority, and consequently no less inferior in official rank, when labouring at Ephesus and Crete, than when attending him in Greece or Asia Minor or Judea.

If any should still think, however, that the supposition of their inferiority is not necessary to explain the tone and contents of these epistles, let them look at the question in another point of view. Let them suppose, though merely for the sake of argument, that these men were not only younger than Paul, and his spiritual children, but inferior in office, and that Paul, in writing to them, had this inferiority in view, and was influenced by it, both in matter and in manner. How could he, without saying *totidem verbis*, you are my inferiors, have more distinctly conveyed that idea than he has done here? What form of address, what selection of topics, what turn of expression, what peculiar tone, what allusions to his own superiority and their subjection to him, could have made the matter clearer than it is? If an air of paternal condescension, if repeated exhortations to fidelity, if positive commands as to official acts, if peremptory orders as to times and places, and express injunctions to return to personal attendance on the writer, do not prove inferiority of rank in those who are addressed, it must be because no proof of the fact is possible, except by formal categorical assertion. If, however, it be true that

Paul addresses these two men precisely as he must have done if they were his inferiors in office, most readers will probably think this a decisive proof that they were so. Nor can it be rejected, without flagrant inconsistency, by those who plead for a perpetual apostleship. The proof of that opinion rests, almost exclusively, upon the fact, that Timothy and Titus are directed to ordain and discipline presbyters, from which it is inferred that they were something more themselves. But if their being thus directed can prove their superiority to elders, how much more does Paul's directing them prove his superiority to them? Those very powers, the imputed exercise of which is made a proof that they were more than presbyters, were exercised at Paul's command, and in conformity with his minute instructions. The least that can be argued from this fact is, that Paul's superiority to Timothy and Titus is as clearly proved as theirs to presbyters. But this is only a small part of the whole truth; for while the proof of their superiority to presbyters is wholly insufficient, that of Paul's superiority to them is perfect. The former, as we have before seen, rests upon the false assumption that a presbyter could neither be ordained nor disciplined by those of the same order. But the fact of Paul's superiority to Timothy and Titus does not rest upon his having ordained them or acted as their judge; but upon his actual control of their official functions, and their actual subjection to his apostolical authority. The very fact of their ordaining and exercising discipline at all may be described as doubtful, in comparison with that of Paul's governing themselves. That they governed and ordained, is a mere inference from Paul's advising them how they should exercise these powers. But that they themselves were ruled by Paul, is no such inference. The fact itself is upon record in these three epistles, which are nothing more nor less than three solemn acts of apostolical authority.

The fact, then, that Timothy and Titus were inferior to Paul in rank and office, is not only upon all common principles of reasoning, but even upon those which are peculiar to the adverse argument, fully established. But if they were inferior to Paul in office, they must either have been presbyters, or something intermediate between that and apostles. The assumption of an intermediate order sweeps away, of course, all arguments to prove that certain persons were apostles, simply because they were superior to presbyters. It also gives a license to assume as many intermediate orders as may be required to demonstrate different hypotheses. In point of fact, however, it is never now assumed. It is one of the conceded points, on which the parties to this controversy meet, that there was no office in the primitive church system, above that of presbyter, exepting the apostleship. If, then, Timothy and Titus were inferior to Paul, they could not have been more than presbyters, and must in that capacity have exercised the right of ordination and of discipline. If, as a last resort, it be alleged, that these powers were exercised by virtue of a special commission, and not as ordinary functions of the eldership, it still remains true, even granting this assertion, that presbyters were competent to exercise these powers, without being elevated to a higher office. What they were thus occasionally authorized to do by the original apostles, they might still do, even if there were apostles in the church; but if, as we shall see hereafter, there are none, then what was occasionally done by presbyters at first, must now be done habitually by them, as the highest class of officers existing, by divine right, in the church. Much more must they possess this right as the successors of the primitive elders, if the latter, as we have the strongest reason to believe, possessed it, not occasionally merely, but as a necessary function of their office.

The result of our inquiry may be briefly stated thus: that Paul addresses the presbyters of Ephesus, as if the whole care of the church was to devolve on them, representing them as shepherds of Christ's flock, a metaphor implying the possession of the highest powers and employed here in its widest sense, because connected with the prediction of dangers which could only be averted by the exercise of great authority, and also because Peter, in addressing the presbyters of Asia Minor, speaks of them as shepherds, subject to no chief shepherd but the Lord Jesus Christ, and possessing powers which might easily become despotic in their exercise. We find too that Paul elsewhere speaks of the presbyters of Ephesus as "ruling," the word employed being one used to denote the government of families, and therefore, in its application to the church, implying the possession of the highest powers, not excepting those of discipline and ordination. And accordingly we find the ordination of Timothy ascribed to a "presbytery," which, on any natural interpretation of the term, can only mean a body of presbyters acting in that character. We find too that Timothy and Titus, while actually exercising the highest powers now belonging to the ministry, are distinctly recognized as Paul's inferiors in rank and office, and therefore as something less than apostles, and nothing more than presbyters, whether acting in the ordinary course of duty, or by virtue of a special commission.

From these special testimonies, singly and together, it appears that presbyters, in apostolic times, possessed and exercised the highest powers now belonging to the ministry. This position having been established by direct proof, it may not be improper to advert to certain passages and detached expressions, which, although they may prove nothing by themselves, and are susceptible of different explanations, and have therefore not been used above in argument, may nevertheless serve as incidental confirmations of the truth already ascertained. One of these is the account of the council at Jerusalem, to which the church of Antioch referred an interesting and important question, sending Paul and Barnabas and others, "unto the apostles AND ELDERS, about this question" (Acts 15 : 2). "And when they were come to Jerusalem, they were received of the apostles AND ELDERS" (v. 4). "And the apostles AND ELDERS came together, for to consider of the matter" (v. 6), and after due deliberation and discussion, "it pleased the apostles AND ELDERS (v. 22) to send a letter to the church at Antioch, with this inscription, "The apostles AND ELDERS and brethren send greeting," etc. (v. 23); and we afterwards read that Paul and Silas, in their missionary tour through Asia Minor, "as they went through the cities, delivered them the decrees for to keep, that were ordained of the apostles AND ELDERS which were at Jerusalem" (Acts 16: 4). All that it is now meant to infer from this transaction is that, even while most of the apostles were still present at Jerusalem, the church there had elders, and that these were not regarded as mere teachers, or leaders in public worship, but as men clothed with authority.

If any should object that the same reasoning would prove the other members of the church to have possessed the same authority, because it was "the church" that received the messengers from Antioch, (Acts 15: 4), because it was "the apostles and elders WITH THE WHOLE CHURCH" that decided the question (v. 22), and because the epistle was written in the name of "the apostles and elders AND BRETHREN," (v. 23), it may be answered, first, that though the brethren, or church at large, are mentioned in these cases, they are not in the others which have been already quoted, whereas the elders are invariably named whenever the apostles are. In the next place, according to the principles of government laid down both in the Old and the New Testament, the church would of course act through the apostles and the elders, and especially the latter, who were really the representatives of the church at Jerusalem, so that it does not even certainly appear, that the church-members were in any sense present except in the person of their representatives; the word translated "multitude" in v. 12 being indefinite and relative in meaning. Lastly, this case is cited only in corroboration of the fact, already proved from other quarters, that the presbyters were rulers, whereas no such proof exists of the powers of government having been exercised by the people generally.

That this constitution of the mother-church was

copied into others, as they were organized, is plain from the practice of Paul and Barnabas, who, as they passed through Asia Minor, "ordained them elders in every church" (Acts 14: 23), and from Paul's leaving Titus in Crete to "ordain elders in every city" (Tit. 1: 5). The powers of these elders were no doubt the same as in the mother-church, and though they are not often mentioned, it is always in a manner to confirm the supposition that they were familiarly regarded as the highest local rulers of the church; as when James says, "Is any sick among you? let him call for the elders of the church" (Jas. 5: 14); and John calls himself, in the inscriptions of two epistles, ὁ πρεσβύτερος; and Peter tells the presbyters of Asia Minor, that he is their fellow-elder (ὁ συμπρεσβύτερος 1 Pet. 5 : 1). That in John's case it denotes the senior apostle, and that in the others it is a generic title for church-officers in general, is no doubt possible; and all that is here intended is to point out how completely even the incidental notices of presbyters agree with the presbyterian hypothesis.

It may be a matter of surprise and even of objection on the part of some, that so few positive testimonies to the truth of that hypothesis are found in Scripture. But let such remember that church-government is very seldom spoken of at all, and ordination scarcely ever, so that in proportion to the space allotted to the general subject, the foregoing proofs may be considered ample. One effect of the comparative neglect of all such matters by the sacred writers is that something, upon any supposition, is to be supplied by inference or analogy. The only question is, which hypothesis requires least to be conjectured or assumed? As this is no unfair criterion of truth, we are willing to submit our doctrine to a rigorous comparison, in this respect, with that of our opponents. They admit that the presbyterial office was established in the primitive church and was intended to be permanent; that it was clothed with the important powers of preaching the gospel and administering the sacraments; and that it is repeatedly spoken of in terms which, taken by themselves, would imply the possession of the highest powers now belonging to the ministry. But this conclusion they avoid by assuming that although the office was intended to continue, and intrusted with some functions of the greatest moment, it was not empowered to ordain or exercise supreme authority, that these prerogatives were specially reserved to a superior order. This, however, cannot be maintained without supposing, that on various occasions when the mention of this higher class would seem to have been almost unavoidable, the sacred writers did nevertheless pass it by in silence, and not only pass it by, but apply the very language that would best describe its powers to the lower order which had no such powers. However this extraordinary fact may be accounted for, it must be assumed, or the adverse doctrine cannot be maintained. The presbyterian hypothesis, on the contrary, takes words and phrases in their usual sense and their most natural construction, and adds nothing to the facts which are admitted by both parties, but setting out from the conceded fact that presbyters were officers of high rank and intrusted with important powers, it concludes that, when they are referred to as the highest local rulers of the churches, they were so in fact; that when certain duties are enjoined upon them, it was meant that they should do them; in a word, that the obvious and natural meaning of the passages which speak of elders is the true one, and that no other need be sought by forced constructions or gratuitous assumptions. By the application of this safe and simple method of interpretation, we have reached the conclusion that presbyters, as presbyters, possessed and exercised the highest ministerial powers, including those of discipline and ordination, in the days of the apostles; that the same rights and powers belong to them at present; and that no ministrations can be charged with invalidity, because they are performed under authority derived from presbyters.

ESSAY III.

ON THE PERPETUITY OF THE APOSTLESHIP.

IN the foregoing essay an attempt was made to prove that the highest permanent office in the church is that of Presbyter, by showing that the primitive Presbyters exercised the highest ministerial functions. In opposition to this doctrine, some allege the superiority and perpetuity of the Apostolic office. If this office was superior to that of Presbyter, and if it was designed to be perpetual, it follows of course that no church authority can rightfully be exercised, except by those who have succeeded the Apostles in the powers which belonged to them as such, and as distinguished from the Elders of the Church. Let it be observed, however; that in order to justify this conclusion, two things must be made out. If the Apostles were not an order of church-officers, distinct from and superior to the Presbyters or Elders, the strongest proof that the office was perpetual only proves that that of Elder was designed to be perpetual, which all admit. If, on the other hand, the Apostolic office was a temporary one, it matters not how far it may have been superior to that held by Presbyters, who still remain, in that case, the highest permanent office-bearers in the Christian Church. In order then to the decision of the controversy, two distinct questions are to be determined. 1. Were the Apostles superior to Presbyters? 2. Was their office, as distinct from that of Presbyter, designed to be perpetual? By some Presbyterian writers both these questions have been answered in the negative, while all Episcopalians, who assert the jus divinum of prelatical episcopacy, answer both affirmatively. In the remainder of the present argument the first point will be conceded; that is to say, it will be granted that the Apostles were church-officers superior to Presbyters or Elders. At the same time an attempt will be made to prove, exclusively from Scripture, that the Apostolic office was a temporary one.

I. The first argument in favour of this proposition is, that the continuance of the office is nowhere expressly stated.

To this it might be answered, that an office being once created, its continuance must be presumed, without an explicit declaration to the contrary.

The general principle is not denied; but in this case there are peculiar circumstances which afford strong ground for a contrary presumption.

1. The original Apostles are uniformly spoken of as constituting a distinct and well defined body of men, not only in the gospel history, but in the latest books of the New Testament. "But beloved, remember ye the words which were spoken before by THE APOSTLES OF OUR LORD JESUS CHRIST, how that they told you there should be mockers in the last time who should walk after their own ungodly lusts" (Jude, vs. 17, 18). This

mode of expression seems to intimate, that "the apostles" belonged to a preceding period, and that most of them were actually gone. Jude could hardly have expressed himself in this way, if the title had already been extended to a multitude of others. "Rejoice over her, thou heaven, and ye holy APOSTLES AND PROPHETS; for God hath revenged you on her" (Rev. 18: 20). Can there be any doubt that this apostrophe is addressed to the original Apostles? And would John have so described them if the name, in his day, had been rightfully assumed by many others, equal and equally "supreme" in power? That he was not familiar with any such extension of the name, may also be inferred from Rev. 21: 14, where he speaks of "the twelve apostles."

It may be urged, however, that the case of Paul destroys the force of the presumption drawn from the mention of the Apostles as a limited number; for he was a thirteenth, and if one might be added, why not more?

This objection would be valid, but for one consideration, which converts the case of Paul into a strong corroboration of the doctrine against which it is alleged. That case is every where referred to and described as an anomalous exception. He speaks of himself as the least of the Apostles (1 Cor. 15: 9), and not only as morally unworthy to be called one, but as almost too late to be an Apostle, as one born out of due time (1 Cor. 15: 8), while at the same time he asserts his equality with the rest as to official rank and power. Now if the Apostolic office was intended to be regularly continued, and if many others were to be brought into it, and invested with its "supreme powers," even during Paul's lifetime, and by his agency, how was he like one born out of due time? Or how could he call himself the least of the Apostles? Can any degree of humility make it consistent with his truth and candour, to pronounce himself inferior, as an Apostle, to Timothy, Titus, Epaphroditus, Silas, Junias, and Andronicus, who were all officially his equals on the opposite hypothesis? Since then the case of Paul is represented by himself as an anomaly, it serves, as a sole exception, to confirm the general statement that the Apostles are referred to as a limited body, not to be increased. This is the first ground of presumption that the office of apostle, as distinguished from all others, was intended to be temporary.

2. A second is, that some of the apostolic powers are acknowledged by both parties in this controversy to have been temporary. The presumption, therefore, is, that all the rest were temporary likewise, except so far as the continuance of any can be clearly shown from Scripture. Now it is not and cannot be denied, that some of them were thus continued, and that for this purpose the offices of Presbyter and Deacon now exist. But this very fact adds greatly to the strength of the presumption, that the apostolic office was a temporary one. For if the cessation of some apostolic powers makes it *a priori* probable that all the rest ceased likewise, how much more does the acknowledged transfer of some of the remaining powers to distinct church-officers, continued in existence for that very purpose, make it *a priori* probable, that all the apostolic powers, which did not thus cease, were thus transferred?

3. The power exercised by the Apostles was a general ambulatory power, not confined to particular districts. This was exactly suited to the infant condition of the church, but could not supersede the necessity of permanent and local officers, after the planting of particular churches. Now the elders and deacons, of whom we read in the New Testament, are the elders and deacons of particular churches, after whose appointment the irregular supervision of the Apostles might be expected to cease, as being no longer needed. On the hypothesis, that the Apostles were commissioned merely to plant the church in various countries, and ordain permanent officers who should exercise such of the apostolical powers as were necessary for the continued existence of the church, while all the others ceased, the course of things could hardly have been different from that which is recorded. This then affords a third ground of presumption that the supposition is coincident with fact.

4. A fourth ground is, that the apostolic functions, which all admit to have been subsequently exercised by Presbyters, are precisely those which, in their own nature, are the most important, namely, the preaching of the gospel and the administration of the sacraments. However important the powers of ordination and discipline may be, they derive their importance from the others. The end of discipline is to preserve purity and exclude the unworthy from the peculiar privileges of the church. The end of ordination is to secure a valid administration of the word and sacraments. If the Head of the Church had left this ministration to any one who chose to perform it, without special ordi-

nation to an office, whatever inconveniences might have attended that arrangement, it could not have impaired the intrinsic value of the word and sacraments. But if, on the other hand, there were no word and sacraments, ordination would be useless. And the same may be said, *mutatis mutandis*, of government or discipline. These then (ordination and discipline) are subsidiary functions which derive their value from the relation they sustain to others. Now if the office of a Christian Presbyter had been invested with powers of a subordinate nature, i. e. such as derive their value from their being necessary to the exercise of others, it might have been alleged, with some degree of plausibility, that the Apostolic office was designed to be perpetual for the sake of those functions which were not bestowed on Presbyters, and yet were essential to the being of the Church. But when we find that the lower office was invested with those powers which possess a necessary and intrinsic value, this, to say the least, adds strength to the presumption that the Apostolic office, which was thus succeeded by another order in its most important functions, was intended to be temporary.

5. On the supposition, that some apostolic powers were neither shared by Presbyters nor discontinued, there is no means of determining what these reserved powers were. For if it be said that all which were not extended to Presbyters were thus reserved, this, in the first place, presupposes the decision of the question whether Presbyters ordained and governed; and, in the next place, supposing that they did not, the successors of the apostles must, according to this rule, possess the power of working miracles, which certainly

belonged to the original apostles. If it be said that this was a temporary gift of an extraordinary nature, then the power of bestowing the Holy Ghost was also temporary. But this many are unwilling to admit. There is, in fact, no unity among Episcopalians, as to the precise powers which have been continued in their Bishops as successors of the Apostles. Some confine their claims to ordination. Some add discipline, as rightfully belonging only to the Bishop. Others add the power of bestowing the Holy Ghost. This last is inseparable from the gift of miracles. Whenever the effects of the gift of the Holy Ghost, conferred by the Apostles, are described, they are of a miraculous nature. The power of bestowing the more inward and spiritual influences of the Holy Ghost, is not only never claimed, but is expressly disclaimed. The Church of Rome is therefore more consistent than the advocates of High Church Episcopacy, in claiming not only the power of conferring the Holy Ghost, but also its inseparable adjunct, that of working miracles. What is here designed, however, is not to disprove the possession of this power, but to show the want of harmony among those who maintain that certain apostolic powers are continued in the church, by means of ministers distinct from and superior to Presbyters. And the design of showing this is to illustrate the impossibility of drawing any line between the powers which ceased or were transferred to Presbyters, and those which are alleged to have been continued in the apostolic office. And the use to be made of this impossibility is simply to strengthen the presumption which has been already raised in favour of the doc trine that the Apostolic office, as distinct from that of Elder and superior to it, was a temporary one.

The grounds of the presumption, then, are, that the twelve apostles are referred to in the New Testament, as a well-known body of men, limited in number, and not to be increased, except in the extraordinary case of Paul, which he himself describes as a remarkable exception; that some of the powers exercised by the original apostles are no longer in existence; that some which still exist are exercised by Presbyters, and were so exercised in apostolic times; that those which are thus exercised by Presbyters are in themselves the most essential to the existence of the church; that the office of Presbyter has been continued in the church for the very purpose of succeeding the apostles in these functions, and with a view to permanent action within fixed local bounds; that the advocates for the perpetuity of the apostolic office are not agreed among themselves as to the powers which now belong to it, and that this want of agreement arises from the silence of Scripture, and the impossibility of fixing any principle, by which a line may be drawn between the powers which are thus continued and those which have ceased or been transferred to Presbyters.

Without insisting on the positive conclusions which might not unreasonably be deduced from these premises, they may be described as furnishing a strong presumption, that the apostolic office was intended to be temporary, bearing the same relation to the permament ministry that a constituent assembly or convention bears to the legislative body which succeeds it. There is presumptive proof of this, so strong that it can only be countervailed by positive evidence from Scripture. The facts, which have been stated as the grounds of this presumption, may be clearly proved from Scripture. It is not too much to ask, then, that if another fact is to be added to the list, viz. that some of the apostolic powers were neither discontinued nor transferred to Presbyters, and that for the exercise of these reserved powers the apostolic office was itself continued, some explicit declaration of the fact may be adduced to countervail the strong adverse presumption. And this brings us back to our first position, that THE CONTINUANCE OF THE APOSTOLIC OFFICE, IN ADDITION TO THOSE WHICH RELIEVED IT OF ITS MOST IMPORTANT FUNCTIONS, IS NOWHERE EXPLICITLY ASSERTED IN THE SCRIPTURES. As the presumptions are so strong against the supposition of a permanent apostleship, the very silence of the Scriptures might be urged as a decisive proof. It cannot be denied, however, that the force of this negative argument would be destroyed by proving that the Scriptures *indirectly* recognize the Apostolic office as perpetual. This leads us to another view of the subject.

II. A second argument in favour of the proposition, that the Apostolic office was a temporary one, is that the name Apostle, in its strict and proper sense, is not applied, in the New Testament, to any persons who were not of the original thirteen.

The passages, in which such an application of the title is alleged, are the following. 1. "But the multitude of the city was divided: and part held with the Jews, and part with THE APOSTLES [meaning Paul and Barnabas]—" which when THE APOSTLES, Barnabas and Paul, heard of, they rent their clothes," etc. (Acts 14: 4, 14).

2. "Salute Andronicus and Junias my kinsmen and my fellow-prisoners, who are of note among THE

APOSTLES, who also were in Christ before me" (Rom. 16 : 7).

3. "Yet I supposed it necessary to send to you Epaphroditus, my brother and companion in labour and fellow-soldier, but your messenger (ἀπόστολον), and one that ministers to my wants" (Phil. 2 : 25).

4. "Whether any do inquire of Titus, he is my partner and fellow-helper concerning you ; or our brethren be inquired of, they are the messengers (ἀπόστολοι) of the churches, and the glory of Christ" (2 Cor. 8 : 23).

5. "Paul and Silvanus and Timotheus unto the church of the Thessalonians" (1 Thess. 1 : 1), compared with "Nor of men sought we glory, neither of you, nor yet of others, when we might have been burdensome AS THE APOSTLES of Christ" (1 Thess. 2 : 6).

From these texts it is inferred by some that Barnabas, Andronicus, Junias, Epaphroditus, Silas, Timothy, and certain brethren who accompanied Titus to Corinth, were Apostles, in the same sense in which Paul was an Apostle; and from this the obvious conclusion has been drawn, that the Apostolic office was intended to be permanent.

It might well be made a question whether the strong antecedent probability, that the Apostolic office was a temporary one, could be wholly set aside by the application of the title in five places, however clear the application might be, and however obvious the sense in which the word is used. The advocates of this interpretation themselves protest against all objections to their system founded merely on the scriptural use of the word *Bishop*, which they own to be convertible with *Presbyter*. They have no right, therefore, to make that of the word *Apostle* the foundation of a perfectly exclusive system. If the *lawfulness* of a superior order were the point in question, incidental proofs of this kind ought to have due weight; but when attempts are made to prove, that the continuance of the Apostolic order, as distinct from that of Presbyters, is essential to the being of a church, and that in the face of such presumptions to the contrary as have been stated, a sober reasoner would have good cause to hesitate before receiving, as conclusive evidence, the application of the name in a few cases, even if the proposed interpretation of the passages referred to were undoubtedly correct.

But this is very far from being certain. Of the five texts cited, there are two, in which the application of the title is at least very doubtful. 1. In the first epistle to the Thessalonians, the word *ἀπόστολοι* is not in juxtaposition or apparent connection with the names of Timothy and Silas, but separated from them by fourteen intervening verses. It is not even alleged, that the joining of other names with Paul's, in the beginning of a letter, makes it necessary to refer the whole of its contents to all the persons thus included in the title; because, after such a joint address, he often uses the first person singular. Nor is it, on the other hand, alleged, that the use of the plural *we* requires such a reference; because that mode of speech is so habitual with Paul, that it may almost be regarded as one of his characteristic idioms; and, as if to guard against such a construction, he says, near the conclusion of this very passage, "Wherefore we would have come unto you, EVEN I PAUL, once and again" (1 Thess. 2: 18). This explanation is, at least, sufficient to outweigh the argument derived from the plural form ἀπόστολοι, which is, no doubt, strictly inapplicable to a single person, but not when preceded, as in this case, by a particle denoting resemblance or comparison. Though Paul could not call himself "the APOSTLES of Christ," he could assert his right to do a thing "AS (i. e. like) the apostles of Christ." He could disclaim having sought glory of them or of others, when he might have been burdensome, AS the apostles of Christ collectively had a right to be. This construction of the sentence is, to say the least, as natural as that which makes the plural form in chap. 2: 6 refer to Timothy and Silas, who are mentioned only in the title (1: 1), and neither there nor elsewhere called apostles.

But even granting that this is a more probable explanation of the plural form, which is a mere gratuitous concession, it would not follow necessarily that Timothy and Titus were Apostles in the sense contended for; because another supposition is still open to us, namely, that ἀπόστολοι is here used in a different sense. For which is it easier to believe, that Silas and Timothy were as much Apostles as Paul himself, but nowhere called so except here by implication and remote allusion; or that when he calls them by that title, he uses it in a wider sense than when it is employed to designate our Lord's immediate followers? We are willing that this question should be answered without any reference to the reasons, hereafter to be stated, for believing that the word *apostle* is employed in a plurality of meanings. Even if there were no other reason for attaching to it a double sense, this case would be just as good a reason for supposing one, as it is for supposing Silas to have been an Apostle, in the absence of all proof from any other quarter. The one argument is this: Paul says, "we, the apostles of Christ," and as Silas and Timothy are mentioned with him in the title of the epistle, they must be included; they were therefore Apostles, in the same sense in which Paul was one. The other argument is this: The Apostles were a limited number, and Paul elsewhere speaks of his addition to it as an extraordinary thing; but Silas and Timothy, though often mentioned, are nowhere else called Apostles; therefore, when Paul so calls them, he uses the title in a wider sense. If these two arguments be only *equal* in conclusive force, they balance one another, and the passage cannot be employed as proof, that Timothy and Silas were "supreme Apostles." This is the case, be it observed, on the supposition that the ἀπόστολοι in ch. 2 : 6 refers to all the men named in ch. 1 : 1. But we have already seen that this reference is doubtful, and that a different construction is, at least, as plausible. The adverse argument, then, rests on two assumptions; that ἀπόστολοι in ch. 2: 6 refers to Timothy and Silas, as well as Paul, and that it must be taken in its strict and highest sense; whereas it is at least as probable that it does not refer to them, and that if it does, it does not denote Apostles in the strict sense. To say the least, then, after every concession, this passage is too doubtful to be made the basis of an argument to prove, in opposition to such strong presumptions, that the office of Apostle was continued.

2. The other case, in which there is a doubt as to the application of the name APOSTLE, is Rom. 16: 7. Here the phrase ἐπίσημοι ἐν τοῖς ἀποστόλοις may mean either *eminent apostles* or *highly esteemed among* (i. e. by) *the apostles.* Admitting, for the sake of argument, that the

former is the better construction, we are not shut up to the conclusion that Andronicus and Junias (or Junia, as Bishop Onderdonk writes it, even while claiming him or her as an apostle) were Apostles in the strict sense. We have just as much reason to believe, that they were Apostles in another sense. Even supposing, for the present, that no such sense of the term can be proved from usage, we have just as much reason to infer it from this passage, as to infer that these two persons were Apostles in the strict sense. For against this inference lies, first, the whole weight of the strong presumption that the apostolic office was a temporary one; and, secondly, the extreme improbability that two eminent apostles, in the strict sense of that title, would be thus named among a crowd of private Christians, and never heard of elsewhere. Is it easier to believe this than that the word apostle has a double meaning, even supposing this to be incapable of proof from any other quarter? We are not now determining the true sense of the passage. We are only showing that a passage which admits, first of two grammatical constructions, and then (assuming that contended for by our opponents) of two interpretations, cannot be regarded as decisive of so difficult and grave a question as the one respecting the perpetual or temporary nature of the apostolic office.

In these two cases, it is doubtful to whom the name Apostle is applied; but in the other three there can be no such doubt. It is admitted that Barnabas, Epaphroditus, and the brethren who accompanied Titus, are expressly called ἀπόστολοι; and from this the inference is drawn by some that the Apostolic office, strictly so called, was conferred upon these persons, and that it consequently did not cease with the original incumbents. This inference involves the assumption that the term *ἀπόστολος* has always the same meaning, namely, that of Apostle in the strict sense, as denoting one of the original thirteen, or a person equal to them in official rank and power, as a ruler of the church under Christ himself. In order to estimate the probability of this assumption, it is necessary to refer to the analogy of other terms, used to denote office in the Christian church.

The other terms admitted, upon both sides, to be so employed are *πρεσβύτερος, ἐπίσκοπος, διάκονος, ποιμήν, διδάσκαλος, προφήτης, ἄγγελος*.* Now let it be observed that, of these seven words, not one was invented for the purpose, or derived from the Hebrew. They are all pure Greek words, used by profane writers, and already familiar to the Jews who spoke that language, before they were appropriated to the use in question. From this state of the case it would be natural and reasonable a priori, to conclude that all the words would have at least a double sense, as used in the New Testament, viz. a wide or popular meaning, according to their etymology and previous usage, and a stricter technical meaning, as appropriated to the designation of ecclesiastical office. How far this natural presumption is confirmed by the actual usage of the New Testament, may be forcibly stated, as to some of these terms, in the words of a well-known episcopal writer.

"Many words have both a loose and a specific meaning. The word 'angel' is often applied loosely

* Εὐαγγελιστής is omitted, because its precise meaning is a matter of dispute. As to the rest, there is a general agreement.

(Acts 12: 15. Rev. 1: 20. 9: 14), but distinctively it means certain created spirits. The word 'God' is applied to angels (Deut. 10: 17. Ps. 97: 7. 136: 2), and idols (Ex. 20: 3. 23: 24, &c.), and human personages or magistrates (Exod. 7: 1. 22: 28. Ps. 82: 1, 6. 138: 1. John 10: 35); but distinctively it means the Supreme Being. The word 'deacon' means an ordinary servant, a servant of God in secular affairs, and any minister of Christ; but a Christian minister of the lower grade is its specific meaning. So with the word 'elder;' it is sometimes applied to the clergy of any grade or grades; but its appropriate application is to ministers of the second or middle order. The above remarks, it is hoped, will enable those who feel an interest in consulting Scripture on the subject before us, to do so without any embarrassment from the apparent confusion of official names or titles."*

"We would also advert to the fact that, however distinct may have been the three above Latin names for the three grades of sacerdotal office, those names of office were, in the Greek, and at an earlier period, applied but loosely. At least, they were so in the New Testament. Thus we read 'this ministry [*deaconship*] and *apostleship* (Acts 1: 25)' for the office to which Matthias was admitted. 'I am the apostle of the gentiles, I magnify mine office' [my *deaconship*], 'the ministry [*deaconship*] which I have received,' 'approving ourselves as the ministers [*deacons*] of God' (Rom. 11: 13. Acts 20: 24. 2 Cor. 6: 4), are passages applied by St. Paul to himself. We also read, 'who then is Paul, and who is Apollos, but ministers [*deacons*] by whom ye believed?' (1 Cor. 3: 5), and 'do

* Episcopacy Examined and Re-examined, p. 14.

the work of an *evangelist*, make full proof of thy ministry [*deaconship*]—thou shalt be a good minister [*deacon*] of Jesus Christ,' are admonitions addressed to Timothy (2 Tim. 4 : 5. 1 Tim. 4 : 6)." "It may not be improper to add some further illustrations of the uncertainty of official names. Thus we say the Jewish 'priesthood,' including in that term, with the priests, the superior order of high priests, and the inferior one of levites. Thus also we have the phrase 'ministry [literally *deaconship*] of reconciliation;' and the expressions, 'that the ministry [*deaconship*] be not blamed;' 'seeing we have this ministry [*deaconship*],' 'putting me into the ministry [*deaconship*],' and more especially 'apostles, prophets, evangelists,' &c., are all said to have been given for the work of the ministry [*deaconship*], (2 Cor. 5: 18. 6: 3. 4: 1. 1 Tim. 1: 12. Eph. 4: 11, 12), in all which passages the word *deaconship*, **διακονία,** the appellation strictly of a sacred body of men, or of their office, includes, nay, signifies chiefly, those who are superior to deacons. The word 'presbytery,' therefore, being no more definite than 'ministry' or 'deaconship,' cannot explain itself in favour of our opponents." "The mere expression *presbytery*, therefore, does not explain itself, and cannot of itself be adduced in favour of parity."*

These quotations from an argument against the doctrine here defended, are not made for the sake of the specific application of an important principle, but for the sake of the principle itself, which is, that names of office "do not explain themselves," and "cannot of themselves be adduced in favour" of either side of the question. An ob-

* Episcopacy Examined and Re-examined, pp. 20, 21.

vious deduction from this rule is, that the bare use of the name "apostle" can prove nothing as to the precise rank of the men to whom it is applied, which can only be determined by a careful collation of the general usage with the context in any given case. Let us proceed to this comparison; but first let us consider the analogous usage of the other titles which have been enumerated, and which are employed to designate ecclesiastical office. In order to secure a satisfactory result, it will be best to survey them *seriatim*.

1. *Πρεσβύτερος* sometimes means *older*, as an adjective in the comparative degree (Luke 15: 25. John 8: 9); sometimes an *old man* in the proper sense (1 Tim. 5: 1, where it is put in opposition to *πρεσβύτερα*); sometimes an officer or magistrate under the Jewish commonwealth (Matt. 21: 23. Mark 15: 1. Luke 7: 3. Acts 4: 8); sometimes an officer of the Christian Church (Acts 15: 2. 20: 17. 1 Tim. 5: 19. Tit. 1: 5. Jas. 5: 14).

2. *Ἐπίσκοπος* (which occurs only five times in the New Testament) is in one case applied to the Lord Jesus Christ as the Head of the Church, or the spiritual guardian of the souls of all believers (1 Peter 2: 25). Elsewhere it denotes the official overseer of a particular church or congregation (Acts 20: 28. Phil. 1: 1. 1 Tim. 3: 2. Tit. 1: 7).

3. *Διάκονος* sometimes means a menial servant, a domestic (Matt. 20: 26. 22: 13. 23: 11. John 2: 5, 9); sometimes a minister or agent either of good or evil (Gal. 2: 17. 2 Cor. 11: 15); sometimes a secular representative of God (Rom. 13: 4); sometimes a minister of the old dispensation (Rom. 15: 8); sometimes a minister of the Christian Church generally, without regard

to rank (2 Cor. 3 : 6. 11 : 23. Eph. 3 : 7. 6 : 21. Col. 1 : 7, 23, 25. 4 : 7. 1 Thess. 3 : 2. 1 Tim. 4 : 6); sometimes a *deacon*, the lowest order of church-officers (Phil. 1 : 1. 1 Tim. 3 : 8, 12).

4. *Ποιμήν* sometimes means a literal shepherd (Matt. 25 : 32. Luke 2 : 8, 15, 18, 20); sometimes a spiritual pastor, both in reference to Christ himself (Matt. 26 : 31. John 10 : 2, 11, 12, 14, 16. Heb. 13 : 20. 1 Pet. 2 : 25), and to his ministers (Eph. 4 : 11).

5. *Διδάσκαλος* sometimes means a teacher generally, as opposed to a learner or disciple (Matt. 10 : 25. Rom. 2 : 20); sometimes a public teacher of religion (Luke 2 : 46. John 3 : 2, 10. Heb. 5 : 12. James 3 : 1), especially the founder of a school or sect (Matt. 9 : 11. 17 : 24. Luke 18 : 18); sometimes an official teacher in the Christian Church (Acts 13 : 1. 1 Cor. 12 : 28, 29. Eph. 4 : 11. 1 Tim. 2 : 7. 2 Tim. 1 : 11. 4 : 3).

6. *Προφήτης* once means a poet, regarded by the heathen as inspired (Tit. 1 : 12). Elsewhere it means, sometimes a prophet of the old dispensation (Matt. 1 : 22. 8 : 17, etc.), sometimes an inspired teacher in the Christian Church (Acts 13 : 1. 1 Cor. 12 : 28, 29. 14 : 29, 32, 37. Eph. 4 : 11).

7. *Ἄγγελος* sometimes means a human messenger (Luke 9 : 52); sometimes a spirit, good or bad (Matt. 1 : 20. 25 : 41. Rev. 3 : 5); sometimes an ecclesiastical superior (Rev. 1 : 20. 2 : 1, 8, 12, 18. 3 : 1, 7, 14).

Now if *ἀπόστολος* has one invariable meaning in the New Testament, it is contrary, not only to what might have been expected from the origin and previous usage of the term, but also to the analogy of the other terms used in the New Testament, to designate ecclesiastical office The only probable supposition *a priori* is, that it would have the same variety of meaning as the rest. Now of the seven terms, which we have been considering, the three which occur most frequently in application to ecclesiastical office, have a threefold usage perfectly distinguishable. They are all used in a popular sense, in a general religious sense, and in a specific ecclesiastical sense. Thus *πρεσβύτερος* is used, in a popular sense, to signify an old man; in a general religious sense, to signify a minister of any rank; and in a strict ecclesiastical sense to signify a presbyter. The popular sense of *διάκονος* is a servant, its more restricted sense a minister, its most restricted sense a deacon. The widest sense of *διδάσκαλος* is a teacher of any kind; its more restricted sense a religious teacher; its most restricted sense, an authorized official teacher in the Christian Church. The three corresponding senses of the word *ἀπόστολος* would be: a messenger of any kind; a religious messenger or missionary; an apostle in the strict official sense before described. And this distinction, suggested by analogy, is verified by usage. The first of these senses occurs in John 13:16, "the servant is not greater than his lord, neither he that is sent (*ἀπόστολος*) greater than he that sent him." Here *ἀπόστολος* stands in the same relation to the *sender*, as the *servant* to the *lord*. The second sense occurs in Rom. 11:13, where *ἐθνῶν ἀπόστολος* means not merely a Christian teacher of the highest rank, but one *sent out* as a missionary to the heathen. The same idea is still more clearly expressed in 1 Tim. 2:7, where the collocation of the words connects *ἀπόστολος*, in a peculiar manner, with *κήρυξ* and *διδάσκαλος ἐθνῶν*. The very same form of speech is repeated in 2 Tim. 1:11. In neither of these cases would the word *bishop*, in the modern sense, seem natural in such a position. If ἀπόστολος is here used in the technical sense, without any special reference to its etymology, why is it thus twice placed between the titles *preacher* and *teacher of the Gentiles?* These remarks are not designed to show, that Paul was not an Apostle in the strict sense, but that the word is sometimes used with special reference to its etymology, and in its secondary sense of a religious messenger or missionary. The third or strict sense is the usual one, and need not be exemplified.

Let us now apply this usage of the term to the three cases which remain to be considered. 1. It appears from Phil. 4 : 10–18, that the Philippian Christians had sent a present to Paul at Rome, by the hands of Epaphroditus. For this act of benevolence the apostle heartily commends and thanks them in the passage just referred to. It is a certain fact, then, that Epaphroditus was a *messenger* from them to Paul, for the specific purpose of supplying his necessities. When, therefore, in a former part of the same letter (ch. 2 : 25) Epaphroditus is described in these terms, "Epaphroditus, my brother and companion in labour and fellow-soldier but your ἀπόστολος," which is more probable, that it means an Apostle in the strict sense, or a messenger? The solution of this question is made still more easy by the words which are added—λειτουργὸν τῆς χρείας μου—which are clearly explanatory of ὑμῶν δὲ ἀπόστολον. This interpretation of ἀπόστολος not only deducts one from the alleged proofs of an addition to the number of apostles, but adds one to the proofs that ἀπόστολος is sometimes used in the sense of messenger.

2. It appears from 2 Cor. 8: 16—22, that Titus, in compliance with Paul's request and his own strong inclination, was about to visit Corinth, and that Paul sent with him "the brother whose praise was in the gospel throughout all the churches," and also another "brother, whom (says he) we have oftentimes proved diligent in many things, but now much more diligent upon the great confidence which I have in you." Of these two persons who accompanied Titus, one is expressly said to have been "chosen of the churches to travel with us [i. e. Paul], with this grace which is administered by us, to the glory of the same Lord and declaration of your ready mind." He was therefore a messenger of the churches, and both he and the other companion of Titus were messengers of Paul to the church at Corinth; and the other would even seem, from the last clause of v. 22, to have been a messenger from that church to Paul. These facts afford sufficient data for the decision of the question as to the sense of the word ἀπόστολοι in the following sentence. "Whether any do inquire of Titus, he is my partner and fellow-helper concerning you; or our brethren be inquired of, they are the ἀπόστολοι of the churches, and the glory of Christ" (2 Cor. 8 : 23). Here are two cases, then, in which the word is applied to persons, who are not known to have been bishops, but who are known to have been messengers, and are so described in the context. This prepares us for the only remaining case, that of Barnabas.

3. Acts 14 : 4, 14. In order to understand this case aright, it is necessary to bear in mind the nature of the work, in which Paul and Barnabas were then engaged. This may be stated in the words of a fa-

vourite episcopal writer. "That this transaction at Antioch [Acts 13: 1] related only to a special missionary 'work,' will be found sufficiently clear by those who will trace Paul and Barnabas through that work, from Acts 13: 4 to 14: 26; where its completion is recorded—'and thence sailed to Antioch from whence they had been recommended to the grace of God for the *work* which they fulfilled.' This 'work,' their missionary tour, being 'fulfilled,' all was fulfilled that had been required by the Holy Ghost, when he had them 'separated' or 'recommended to the grace of God' 'for the work to which he had called them.' This call, therefore, this separation, this 'work,' related only to a particular mission. And this laying on of hands was no ordination, but a lesser ceremony, which has no bearing on the controversy between parity and episcopacy." "When the latter [i. e. Barnabas] had been made an Apostle, we know not; neither do we know when James the brother of the Lord, Sylvanus, etc., were admitted to that office."*

The case then stands thus: two men are called ἀπόστολοι, one of whom we know to have been an Apostle in the highest sense; but when the other "had been made an Apostle, we know not." From this application of the term our opponents infer that both were Apostles in the strict sense. To this we might reply that Barnabas is here called an Apostle in the strict sense, or rather included in the term ἀπόστολοι—for he is never so called separately, although often mentioned, and several times described (Acts 4: 36. 9: 27. 11: 24. 13: 1. 15: 35)—merely because he was Paul's colleague in this work, just as Silas is included

* Episcopacy Examined and Re-examined, pp. 17, 18.

in the description of "Roman citizens" (Acts 16 : 37, 38), for no reason that appears but his connection with Paul, who is expressly and repeatedly declared to have been a Roman citizen (Acts 22 : 25, 26, 27, 29. 23 : 27). Even granting, therefore, that ἀπόστολος is here used in its strict sense, it is by no means certain that it could have been applied, in that sense, to Barnabas alone; the rather as we have found no other case, in which it is so applied, either to him or any other person not of the original thirteen.

So too on the other hand, even admitting that he is individually styled an ἀπόστολος, it does not follow that he is so styled in the strict sense of the term. The word, as we have seen, is used to denote three things—(1) a messenger of any kind—(2) a religious messenger or missionary—(3) an apostle in the strict sense. The name is here applied to a man who is nowhere else called an apostle or described as one, but who was, at the very time referred to, engaged with Paul in "a special missionary work," a "missionary tour," to which the Holy Ghost had called them; for "this call, this separation, this work, related only to a particular mission." Under these circumstances, which is more probable, that ἀπόστολος, as thus used, means a *missionary*, or that it means a supreme ruler of the church, equal in rank to the original thirteen? If it means the latter, it is singular, to say the least, that Barnabas, who is so often mentioned and repeatedly described, is nowhere else called an Apostle, which, in the case supposed, was his grand distinction. But if, on the other hand, he is so called in the lower sense, it is easy to explain why he is nowhere else so called, to wit, because his apostolic character was temporary.

"This work, this missionary tour, being fulfilled, all was fulfilled that had been required by the Holy Ghost, when he had them separated or recommended to the grace of God, for the work to which he had called them. This call, this separation, this work, related only to a particular mission." True, he afterwards went out upon a similar mission, but not, as it would seem, under church authority, nor is the narrative of that mission upon record. Paul, on the contrary, was still an Apostle, and is still so called, which makes it at least probable that he was an Apostle in a higher sense than Barnabas.

Still it may be argued that as both are called Apostles, and as Paul was certainly one in the highest sense, the inference is plain that Barnabas was also an Apostle in the highest sense. This would be valid reasoning if it were not equally certain that Paul was an Apostle in the lower sense too. One of the senses of the word applies to both; another applies certainly to one of them. Which is more reasonable, to infer that the latter applied also to the other, or to infer that the former is the sense here intended? In the one case, this solitary passage is adduced to prove what is nowhere else recorded, viz. that Barnabas was strictly an Apostle. In the other case, nothing is assumed or supposed to be here proved, but what is clearly revealed elsewhere, viz. that both Barnabas and Paul were missionaries.

The argument admits of a familiar illustration. In the foreign missions of our own and other churches, the word "missionary" has a double sense; a strict one applicable only to ordained ministers or clergymen, and a wider one including lay-assistants. The first is considered the most proper, and is certainly the most usual sense; but the other does undoubtedly occur, even in the official documents of missionary boards, especially when several or all of those engaged in the work are spoken of collectively. Let us suppose then that in a certain mission two persons, A and B, have long been labouring, the first as a preacher, the second as a lay-assistant, but that in some one report or journal they are twice mentioned by the common name of *missionaries*, and it becomes a question with some readers of the document, whether B was not an ordained minister. On examining the series of reports and journals, it is found that B is nowhere else even called a missionary, and that in the case in question no act is ascribed to him which necessarily implies that he is an ordained minister. From these premises two opposite inferences are drawn. The one is, that as A is certainly a clergyman, and as both are called missionaries, B must be a clergyman also. The other is, that as B is nowhere else represented as a clergyman, and as both he and A are certainly missionaries in a wider sense, that is the sense in which the term is used. Without insisting on a choice between these opposite deductions, as entirely conclusive, we may ask what would be thought of an argument to prove a doubtful point, as to the organization of the mission, from the mere application of the term in such a case? But in the case of Barnabas there is this distinctive circumstance, that the antecedent probability is in favour of the supposition, that the apostolic office, in the strict sense, was confined to a certain number of persons, among whom Barnabas was not; and that this presumption can only be removed by positive proof that he was an Apostle.

The amount, then, of the argument from names is this, that of five cases, in which the name apostle is said to be applied to persons not of the original thirteen, there are two in which the application is itself disputed, and at least so far doubtful as to render them unfit to be relied on as proofs; while in these cases, and in all the rest, the word either requires or admits another sense than that of an Apostle proper. These cases, therefore, make no change in the truth of the general proposition, that the extension of the Apostolic office to persons not of the original thirteen, is nowhere taught in Scripture, either directly, by explicit assertion of the fact, or indirectly, by the application of the name Apostle, in its strict and highest sense.

III. A third argument in favour of the proposition, that the Apostolic office was a temporary one, is that the qualifications for the Apostleship, as a permanent office in the church, are nowhere stated. Even supposing that an explicit statement of the fact might easily have been omitted, which is not the case, and that the absence of any unequivocal application of the name may be accounted for, which seems impossible, the question still arises, why are the qualifications of an "Apostle-bishop" not revealed? It is not enough to say, because Paul or Peter has not left epistles to those who were to consecrate Apostle-bishops. Granting the fact, why was not such a revelation made? Were the instructions to Timothy and Titus, as to "Presbyter-bishops," given without necessity? If not, why was not an occasion sought or made for giving the qualifications of Apostles? Because this office demands none in particular, or because it is less important than the others? It may be said, indeed, that we have no right to inquire why certain things have been revealed and others not. But this would be a mere evasion of the argument by the misapplication of an acknowledged principle. The question is not what should have been, but what has been revealed; and if both parties are agreed that certain offices are recognized in the New Testament, and the qualifications for those offices carefully detailed, and if one of the parties alleges that another office is there recognized, the other party has a right to ask how the omission of its qualifications is to be explained upon the opposite hypothesis. This would be the case, even if the disputed office were the lowest. If, for example, the qualifications of Deacons had nowhere been given, the evidence of such an office, as a permanent order in the church, would be much less conclusive than that of the Presbyterate, although Deacons are expressly mentioned, in connection with the Presbyters or Bishops, in two of Paul's epistles. How much inferior, then, is the evidence that Apostles were permanent officers of the church, when both these proofs are wanting! And how much weaker still when we consider the paramount importance attached to the apostolic office by the adverse party!

Even admitting, then, that no occasion does present itself in the New Testament, as it stands, for the detail of the qualifications of Apostles, that very circumstance increases, in a high degree, the improbability that such an office was intended to be permanently established. But this admission is gratuitous. By whom were subsequent apostles to be consecrated, if not by their predecessors in the office? If, then,

Timothy and Titus were apostles, and addressed as such in Paul's epistles, why does he not instruct them in relation to the paramount importance of admitting only qualified men to that high station? Is it because the same qualifications which are required in presbyters are also required in apostles? Even if this were so, the great alleged superiority of the apostolic office would entitle it to the honour of a separate enactment, especially as presbyters and deacons are distinctly treated, though the qualifications for these two offices are almost identical. This difficulty is not merely theoretical, but practical; for how are the qualifications of Apostle-bishops now to be determined? By what test shall they be judged? Those described in the first chapter of Acts are totally inapplicable to all modern cases. How then is it to be ascertained whether those admitted now to the alleged rank of Apostles are as certainly possessed of the necessary qualifications as Presbyters and Deacons, who are tried by the directions which Paul gave to Timothy and Titus? It is not pretended that this omission is itself sufficient to disprove the perpetuity of the Apostolic office, but merely that it renders it so far improbable as to require the most explicit proof to establish it.

But even this is not a full view of the subject of apostolical qualifications. It is not only true that no account is given of the qualifications of Apostle-bishops, as permanent officers in the church, after it had been planted by the original Apostles; but also that the qualifications which are given of an original Apostle are of such a nature as to discountenance, in a high degree, the opinion that the office was intended to be permanent. When the death of Judas made a vacancy in the apostolic body, the disciples proceeded to elect a successor, and Peter, in the name of the eleven, declared the qualifications which were requisite. These were, first, that the candidate should have been one of Christ's original followers; secondly, that he should be a witness of the resurrection (Acts 1:21, 22). The obvious *prima facie* inference from this is certainly that none could be apostles who were destitute of these qualifications. And this is very much confirmed by the case of Paul, who seems not to have known the Saviour personally, during his abode on the earth, but who, in vindicating his own claim to an equality of rank with the eleven, says expressly, "Have I not seen the Lord Jesus?"—thereby admitting that to have seen him was necessary to the apostolic character. This might be urged, with plausibility at least, as a direct proof that the Apostolic office was a temporary one, because the number of those who had actually seen Christ after his resurrection was limited, and must soon be exhausted. All that is now alleged, however, is that the absence of express declarations that the Apostolic office was continued in the church, is the more difficult to be explained on the opposite hypothesis, because when the qualifications of church-officers are given, in two separate epistles, those of Apostles are not included; and because the only requisites prescribed in the election of a man to fill a vacancy in the original apostolic body, are precisely such as cannot be possessed by any men at present.

It may, however, be alleged, that although the permanence of the apostolic office is not explicitly asserted, and although the qualifications of Apostle-bishops are not given, and although the name Apostle, in its highest sense, is not applied to any but the original thirteen; others are, nevertheless, spoken of as actually exercising apostolic powers, and that as it is the thing, and not the name, which is really in question, this is sufficient to establish the perpetuity of the Apostleship. Before proceeding to examine the grounds of this allegation, there are two preliminary observations to be made upon it.

1. The omission of the name Apostle is by no means an unimportant circumstance. The title was not so regarded in the original institution. It did not grow out of circumstances, nor was it, in any sense, the result of accident. It is not said, in an incidental way, that the twelve were called apostles, as it is said that the disciples were called Christians at Antioch; but we are told, that our Lord "called unto him his disciples, and of them he chose twelve, whom also HE NAMED APOSTLES" (Luke 6 : 13). The office and the name were conferred by the same authority. When the persons thus chosen are afterwards mentioned, it is commonly by the name which Christ bestowed at first, or by that of "the twelve," denoting their limited number. After our Lord's ascension, there seems to be no instance of the Apostles, in the strict sense, being called by any indefinite name. Now these two facts, that the name was coeval with the office and recorded as a matter of some moment, and that the original Apostles are almost always, and after Christ's ascension always, called by it or some other title equally definite, render it *a priori* highly probable, that if the office was to be continued, the name would be continued with it; and that if continued in common parlance, it

would be applied in the New Testament; and that if applied at all, it would be applied with greater frequency than ever after the name had been extended to a multitude of persons. How is it that as the number of apostles increased, the mention of the name becomes less frequent, even when the organization of the church and the qualifications of its officers are the subject of discourse? These considerations will perhaps suffice to show, that the failure to establish the explicit application of the name Apostle to the alleged successors of the original thirteen is by no means a matter of indifference, even if it can be shown that they possessed and exercised apostolic powers. Not that the actual possession and exercise of peculiar apostolic powers does not prove them to have been apostles; but the omission of the title makes it harder to establish the fact of such possession and exercise, and entitles us to call for more explicit proof than might otherwise be necessary.

2. Before the exercise of apostolic powers by persons not of the original thirteen can be adduced in proof of the permanent continuance of the apostolic office, it must be determined what are apostolic powers. It cannot mean all the powers of the original apostles; for some of these are admitted, on both sides, to have ceased. It cannot mean any of these powers indefinitely; for some of them are admitted, on both sides, to be lawfully exercised by presbyters; and this would prove that presbyters are the successors of the apostles in the highest of their powers which did not cease. If the possession of any apostolic powers is a proof of the succession, then the succession is in presbyters. If the possession of all the apostolic powers is

necessary to establish a succession, then there is none at all. Either of these conclusions would be fatal to the adverse argument, which cannot have the slightest force, except on two conditions; first, that the apostolic powers, shown to have been exercised by persons not of the original thirteen, be such as are not acknowledged to have ceased; and then, that they be such as were not exercised by Presbyters. For if they were powers possessed by Presbyters, their exercise proves nothing but the continuance of that office, which is not disputed; and if they were powers which have ceased, their exercise in apostolic times proves nothing as to the rights and powers of any office now existing in the church.

ESSAY IV.

ON THE OFFICIAL RANK OF TIMOTHY AND TITUS.

I HAVE endeavoured to show that the Apostolic office was not meant to be perpetual; first, because the continuance of the office is nowhere explicitly asserted; secondly, because the name Apostle, in its strict and proper sense, is not applied in the New Testament to any who were not of the original thirteen; thirdly, because the qualifications for the Apostleship, as a permanent office in the church, are nowhere stated.

A fourth argument against the perpetuity of the Apostolic office is, that no peculiar apostolic powers are said in Scripture to have been exercised by any person, who was not either an original Apostle or a Presbyter.

The only cases commonly alleged by controversial writers on this subject are those of Timothy and Titus, and the allegation, even with respect to them, is not founded on the historical statements of the New Testament, but on the instructions given them by Paul, in his epistles addressed to them respectively. Let this fact be duly noted and borne in mind, when we examine the proof from the epistles. If, in the Acts of the Apostles, Timothy and Titus appeared as the equals and colleagues of Paul, this would create a presumption in favour of their having been Apostles; and this presumption would materially influence the interpretation of his epistles to them; that is to say, expressions of a dubious import might be fairly interpreted so as to agree with the presumption afforded by the history. But what is the true state of the case in this respect?

The first mention of Timothy is in Acts 16 : 1, where we read that Paul came to Derbe and Lystra, and found a certain disciple there, named Timotheus, the son of a believing Jewess and of a Greek or heathen father. The son was well reported of by the brethren that were at Lystra and Iconium. "Him would Paul have to go forth with him, and took and circumcised him, because of the Jews which were in those quarters, for they all knew that his father was a Greek."

In the subsequent narrative it is hard to tell whether Timothy is represented as performing even ordinary ministerial functions, as Silas was also in Paul's company, and the plural forms of speech employed may be restricted to these two. In the account of the persecution at Philippi (Acts 16: 19—40), Timothy is not mentioned, and in ch. 17: 4, 10, "Paul and Silas" are mentioned without Timothy, who was still in their company, however, as appears from Acts 17: 14, 15. 18: 5. The omission of his name seems to show that he was not so intimately related to Paul, at this time, as Silas was. The office of Timothy would indeed appear to have been precisely that which John Mark sustained in Paul's first mission, namely, that of an ὑπηρέτης, a personal attendant (Acts 13 : 5). And accordingly we find Timothy and Erastus afterwards described by an equivalent expression, δύο τῶν διακονούντων αὐτῷ (Acts 19 : 22). They are called *ministers*, not of God (2 Cor. 6 : 4), not of Christ (2 Cor. 11 : 23), not of the gospel (Eph. 3 : 7), not of the New Testament (2 Cor. 3 : 6), not of the church (Col. 1 : 52), but of Paul, i. e. personal attendants on him. Or if they were *ministers* in a higher sense, their relative position, with respect to Paul, was that of διάκονοι to an official superior. Timothy next appears as the fifth in the list of Paul's companions on his return from Greece to Syria (Acts 20 : 4), in which list Silas, Paul's colleague in the mission, is not included. These are all the traces which we find of Timothy in the Acts of the Apostles; and in these, he acts no other part than that of an attendant upon Paul.

That he became a minister, a διάκονος in the higher sense, a presbyter, a preacher of the gospel, is admitted. Hence in the epistle to the Romans (16 : 21), Paul speaks of him as his "work-fellow," a title, however, which would not have been inapplicable to him, even as a lay attendant. In the first epistle to the Corinthians, he mentions him twice, once as his "beloved son and faithful in the Lord" (ch. 4 : 17), and again as "one that worketh the work of the Lord as I also do" (ch. 16 : 10). That this does not imply official equality between them as Apostles, is clear, because the terms are perfectly applicable to the ordinary work of the ministry; because the phrase "worketh the work of the Lord" is more applicable to the ordinary work of the ministry than to peculiar apostolic functions; and because in this very epistle (ch. 4 : 17.

16 : 10, 11), Paul directs the movements of Timothy, as those of an inferior.

In the second epistle to the Corinthians, Timothy is mentioned in the title as follows: "Paul an Apostle of Jesus Christ by the will of God, and Timothy the brother." If Timothy had been then an Apostle, could there have been a more appropriate occasion so to call him? Could it well have been avoided? And if the mention of his apostolic character had been neglected once, could the omission be repeated as it is in the title of Colossians? It may indeed be said that in the title of the epistle to Philemon, Paul is called "a prisoner of Jesus Christ" and Timothy "a brother," whereas both were prisoners. But in Heb. 13 : 23, an epistle of the same date, it is said, "know ye that our brother Timothy is set at liberty. Besides, δέσμιος is no title of office like ἀπόστολος.

This argument from the use of the word "brother," where "Apostle" might have been expected, has been very summarily set aside as follows. "Why does Paul in some places call himself an Apostle, and Timothy only a brother? . . . . Really it is too late to inquire; but the fact has not the least bearing on the point in question. The Apostles were brethren to each other, the elders were brethren to the Apostles, so were the deacons; so were the laity. The circumstance, therefore, of Paul's calling Timothy a brother, while he calls himself an Apostle, proves no more that Timothy was not an Apostle, than it does that he was not a clergyman at all, but only a layman."*

This explanation takes for granted, that the argument, to which it is an answer, depends for its

* Episcopacy Examined and Re-examined, p. 50.

validity upon the meaning of the word ἀδελφός, which is not the case. The argument is not that Timothy was no Apostle because Paul calls him a brother, but because Paul does not call him an Apostle when he calls himself one. The case would have been substantially the same, if any other title had been given to Timothy, or none at all. If, for example, he had said, "Paul an Apostle of Jesus Christ, and Timothy," the inference would still have been that Timothy was no Apostle, not because Paul describes him as being something else, but because he does not describe him as being an Apostle, in the very circumstances where such a description, if consistent with the fact, would seem to be unavoidable. It matters not, then, how vague or indecisive the term "brother" may be, in itself considered, or when separately used. If Paul had merely called Timothy "a brother," the term would have had no distinctive meaning; but when put in opposition to "apostle," it becomes distinctive, as in Acts 15 : 23, where "apostles, presbyters, and brethren" are enumerated. Are not three distinct classes here intended? Yet "the apostles were brethren to each other, the elders were brethren to the apostles, so were the laity." But the vague term *brethren*, when connected with the specific titles *apostles* and *elders*, itself acquires a specific meaning.

That this is the case in Acts 15 : 6, 23, may be proved by the same high authority which denies it in the case before us. "These two classes of ministers are distinguished from each other in the passages which speak of them as 'apostles *and* elders,' or which enumerate 'apostles *and* elders *and* brethren,' or the laity. If 'priests *and* levites,' if 'bishops *and* deacons,' are allowed to be distinct orders, if 'apostles *and* brethren' are also allowed to be distinct orders, then on the same principle that the conjunction is not exegetical, 'apostles *and* elders' may fairly be accounted distinct orders likewise. And as in the expression 'apostles *and* elders *and* brethren' severalty is unquestionably implied between the latter of these three classes and the others, it must as clearly be implied between the former two. Apostles were therefore one class, and elders another class, just as the laity were a third class."*

There seems to be no reason why the principle thus clearly and correctly stated in relation to the plural forms "apostles and brethren," should not apply to the singular forms "apostle and brother." If it be said that in the latter case, ἀδελφός is not the specific designation of a class, as ἀδελφοί is in the other, it may be replied that ἀδελφοί owes its specific meaning to its combination with two other terms of office. This may be rendered clear by supposing that certain persons had been mentioned in Acts xv. as οἱ ἀδελφοί simply, without the use of any other title. The term would then be perfectly indefinite, and we should be left to gather from the context or to guess whether it signified apostles, or apostles and elders, or the whole body of believers. But when employed in combination with the other terms, it necessarily acquires a distinct sense analogous to them. Why then is not the same effect produced upon the meaning of the singular ἀδελφός by its combination with the singular ἀπόστολος? It is not disputed that the latter is as much a name of office as ἀπόστολοι in Acts xv. There is no reason therefore

* Episcopacy Examined and Re-examined, pp. 14. 15.

for supposing that ἀδελφός is not as distinctive in its meaning as ἀδελφοί.

The perfect analogy between the cases will be clear if we advert to the grammatical principle on which the general expression *brethren*, as used in Acts, acquires a specific meaning. Since the name, in itself, was applicable to the apostles and presbyters as well as the lay-brethren, it would embrace them all unless its meaning had been limited by the express mention of two classes comprehended under the generic term. That is to say, the name ἀδελφοί comprehends apostles, presbyters, and private Christians, and when used alone might be naturally understood to signify them all. But when either of those classes is expressly mentioned by its proper title, the general term, if still used, must of course be used to signify the rest. Thus "apostles and elders and brethren" means "apostles and elders (who are not apostles) and brethren (who are neither apostles nor elders)." So too "an apostle and a brother" means "an apostle and a brother (who is not an apostle)." Or if it does not, some reason should be given for the use of an expression which seems just as distinctive as the one in Acts.

I have said, however, that the strength of the argument does not depend upon the meaning of ἀδελφός, and that even if that word had been omitted, the natural inference would still have been that Timothy was no Apostle. This admits of illustration from analogy. When Cicero and Antony were consuls, it is scarcely conceivable that a joint official letter from them could have been inscribed as follows: "M. T. Cicero Consul et M. Antonius Civis Romanus." Such an inscription would have been universally regarded as presumptive evidence that the Antony thus mentioned was not at the time consul; a presumption capable of being removed, but only by positive proof of the most conclusive kind, including the assignment of some reason for the obvious distinction drawn between the colleagues. But why should such proof be required? The terms of the inscription would be absolutely true, even if Antony was consul; for both he and his colleague were Roman citizens, and there is nothing inconsistent with the fact in giving Cicero a specific name and Antony a generic one. All this is true, and yet it would be wholly inconclusive for this reason, that the inference, as to Antony's not being consul, was not founded on the truth or falsehood of the title *civis*, nor on its general or specific sense, but on the unaccountable distinction drawn between him and his colleague, by the marked application of the official title to one of them exclusively.

This view of the matter serves to show the fallacy involved in the assertion that "Paul's calling Timothy a brother, while he calls himself an Apostle, proves no more that Timothy was not an Apostle than it does that he was not a clergyman at all, but only a layman." The inference that Timothy was no Apostle is deduced from the distinction so expressly made between him and Paul as an Apostle. There is no such distinction made between him and Paul as a clergyman or minister, and therefore there is no ground for the inference that Timothy was "only a layman." An argument founded on the express mention of a certain office, however little it may prove as to that office, cannot prove as much, because it can prove nothing, as to an office which is not mentioned at all. If we read, in a Presbyterian publication, of "A. B. the pastor and C. D. a member of the church," although we know that, according to our constitution, pastors are always elders, and elders are always members of the church, we should certainly infer, with absolute certainty, that C. D. was not a collegiate pastor with A. B., nor would our confidence in this conclusion be at all impaired by being told, that the writer's calling C. D. a church-member no more proved that he was not a pastor than it proved that he was not an elder. If again we read, in an Episcopal journal, of "Bishop Potter and Dr. Dorr," we should certainly regard the very form of the expression as sufficient to evince that Dr. Dorr was not Assistant Bishop of Pennsylvania, even in spite of the assurance that the terms used no more prove that Dr. D. is not a bishop, than they prove that he is not a presbyter, because bishops, presbyters, deacons, and even laymen, may be doctors. In both these cases, as in that which they are used to illustrate, every reader feels that, if the higher title belonged equally to both the persons mentioned, its being applied to one, and not the other, would be an anomaly requiring explanation, in default of which the inference seems unavoidable, that the application was designed to be exclusive; or, in other words, that when Paul, in two epistles, calls himself an apostle and Timothy a brother, he excludes the latter from the rank of an apostle.

In the epistle to the Philippians (2:19–23) we find Paul proposing to send Timothy to them, and describing him as one like-minded, who would naturally care for their state, who had served with Paul in the gospel, as a son with a father. These expressions are not only reconcilable with the supposition, that Timothy, although a presbyter, was Paul's inferior and under his direction, but agree far better with that supposition than with the supposition that he was Paul's equal, a "supreme" Apostle. In the epistles to the Thessalonians, Silas (or Silvanus) and Timothy are joined with Paul in the inscriptions. It has never been contended that this of itself implies equality of rank; and that it does not, is sufficiently apparent from 1 Thess. 3:2, where Paul again appears directing Timothy's movements, and where Timothy is described as a brother, a minister of God, a fellow-labourer in the gospel of Christ, but not as an Apostle. And yet here, if anywhere, the introduction of that title would have been not only natural, but almost unavoidable, had Timothy been really entitled to it.

These are all the cases in which Timothy is mentioned, except in the epistles addressed to himself, and from a view of the whole it would appear, that in the history he is mentioned only as a personal attendant upon Paul; that in the epistles, he appears as a minister of God, a preacher of Christ, a fellow-labourer of Paul in the gospel, all which expressions are applicable to him as a presbyter, and cannot therefore furnish any proof that he was an Apostle; that he is never expressly called an Apostle, even when he is particularly mentioned and described, and when the omission of the title could not fail, on any ordinary principle of interpretation, to distinguish him from Paul who is described as an Apostle; that while he is nowhere represented as performing apostolic acts, he is repeatedly described as being subject to Paul's orders and directions, a fact which harmonizes perfectly with the supposition of his official inferiority, and can only be reconciled with any other by means of forced constructions and gratuitous assumptions. This view of Timothy's official character, as it appears in the other epistles and the Acts of the Apostles, will prepare us for the consideration of the two epistles to himself, and for the question, whether these epistles contain proof of his apostleship so clear as to invalidate the strong presumption, that he was officially inferior to Paul.

In the title or inscription of the first epistle, Paul addresses Timothy as his "own son in the faith," and in that of the second as his "dearly beloved son." These epithets prove nothing, as to official rank or power, and are only remarkable as additional instances of the consistent uniformity with which the name Apostle is withheld from Timothy, whether in speaking to or of him.

From 1 Tim. 1: 3, it appears that, when Paul went into Macedonia, he left Timothy in Ephesus, that he might "charge some to teach no other doctrines, neither give heed to fables," etc. This charge he is again said, in v. 18, to have committed to Timothy, according to the prophecies which went before upon him. The phrase "this charge" must refer either to the "ministry" which Paul himself had received, according to v. 12, or to the charge mentioned in v. 3. If it means the former, the word *διακονία*, being applicable to all ranks, proves nothing as to Timothy's apostleship. But that it means the latter appears more probable, from the parenthetical character of the whole intervening passage, vs. 5–17, as well as from the verbal correspondence between *παραγγείλῃς* (v. 3) and *παραγγελίαν* (vs. 5, 18).

The second chapter contains directions with respect to public prayer, its subjects (vs. 1–7), the persons permitted to perform it (v. 8), and the duty of women with respect to public worship (vs. 9–15). No personal agency is expressly ascribed to Timothy, but it is evidently implied that he was to enforce these regulations, and of course that he was clothed with power so to do.

The third chapter contains the qualifications of bishops and deacons. Here again no personal agency is ascribed to Timothy. It is said, indeed, in v. 14, "these things write I unto thee, hoping to come unto thee shortly; but if I tarry long, that thou mayest know how to behave thyself in the house of God, which is the church," etc. This might possibly refer to Timothy's own conduct in one of the two offices which had just been described, or in both, for the greater includes the less. But when taken in connection with the "charge" mentioned in ch. 1: 3, 18, it seems to imply that these directions are given to him, because he would be called upon to ordain others, and that he might know what qualifications to require.

In the fourth chapter, after enumerating certain heretical and fanatical errors which were to be looked for, Paul says to Timothy (v. 6), "if thou put the brethren in remembrance of these things, thou shalt be a good minister of Jesus Christ," etc. The "brethren," whom Timothy was thus to "put in remembrance," may have been either brethren in the ministry, or laymen, or the whole Christian brotherhood, including both. In relation to these and some other matters, the Apostle adds, "these things command and teach" (v. 11). He then exhorts him to avoid contempt, by setting an example of consistent conduct, purity, etc., adding "till I come, give attendance to reading, to exhortation, to doctrine" (v. 13). This implies that when Paul did come, he would give him more particular directions for his subsequent conduct, a suggestion which by no means favours, though it may not directly impugn, the hypothesis of Timothy's apostleship. The important passage, 1 Tim. 4: 14, having been examined at length in a former essay, is here omitted.

In ch. 4: 15, Paul exhorts Timothy to meditate on these instructions, and to give himself wholly to his work, that his improvement (προκοπή) might appear to all. This, to say the least, is more in accordance with the supposition, that the person thus addressed was a young preacher, of the common rank, who had a character to form and influence to gain, than that he was a "supreme apostle," the official equal of the person writing. In the next verse (ch. 4: 16) Paul exhorts him to take heed to himself (i. e. his personal deportment and hopes), and to his doctrine (what he preached), and to continue in them, because in so doing he would both save himself and those who heard him. Timothy here appears in the character of a preacher, without any allusion to higher powers than might have belonged to an ordinary presbyter.

In ch. 5: 1, he is told not to rebuke an elder, but entreat him as a father. Even if πρεσβύτερος had here its technical meaning, as a name of office, the passage would prove nothing as to Timothy's official rank, because upon the supposition that he was a presbyter, nothing could be more natural than the exhortation not to rebuke a brother presbyter, but to entreat him. But that πρεσβύτερος is here used in its primary and proper sense, that of an old man, is apparent from the whole drift of the passage, and especially from the antithetical relation which πρεσβυτέρῳ sustains to νεωτέρους in the same verse and πρεσβυτέρας in the next. In v. 7, he is commanded to give these things in charge (πάραγγελλε), which implies that he was vested with authority to reprove and exhort both old and young, and to regulate the conduct of the church towards widows as the object of their charity. The same may be said of v. 11 and the intervening verses, and indeed of the whole passage ending with v. 15.

1 Tim. 5: 17 has been a subject of much controversy, as to the questions whether πρεσβύτεροι means *old men* in the popular, or *elders* in the official sense; and whether a distinction is here recognized between the two classes of teaching and ruling elders. The discussion of these questions would be foreign from my present purpose. Whether ruling elders, as distinct from preachers of the gospel, are here spoken of or not, it is admitted upon all hands that the text relates to presbyters or elders in the highest sense, and it will therefore be sufficient for the present purpose to assume that they alone are mentioned. It appears, then, that Timothy is here directed, at least by implication, to treat certain presbyters with particular respect. This does not necessarily imply that he was their superior; for the very same exhortation might have been addressed to the people, who seem indeed to be included in the exhortation, as the indefinite passive form (ἀξιούσθωσαν) is used, instead of a direct address to Timothy. If Paul, in writing to the whole church, might have said, "Let the presbyters who rule well be counted worthy of double honour," without imply-

ing that the presbyters were subject to the body of the brethren, his use of the same form of speech to Timothy cannot possibly prove that they were subject to him. But one thing it does prove, of a very different nature, to wit, that Presbyters were *rulers* in the church, and not mere agents of "apostle-bishops." It may be said, that προεστῶτες merely means presiding or holding the first place. This is a question to be settled by usage.

In Rom. 12 : 8, ὁ προϊστάμενος cannot denote mere rank or conspicuous position, for two reasons; because a man could not be exhorted to hold such a position "with diligence;" and because all the other terms connected with it denote specific actions. The same thing is evident from the collocation of προϊσταμένους, in 1 Thess. 5 : 12, between κοπιῶντας and νουθετοῦντας, both denoting specific functions of the ministry. In 1 Tim. 3 : 4, Paul requires a bishop to be one that ruleth well (καλῶς προϊστάμενον) his own house, which can hardly mean one who holds the first place in it, without any original jurisdiction over it. The same remark applies to v. 12, where the deacons are described as ruling (προϊστάμενοι) their children and their households well. Let the same sense which προΐστημι evidently has in these four cases, be applied to that before us, and it becomes plain that presbyters are spoken of as ruling just as really as bishops and deacons are said to rule their own families. That the rule referred to is that of the church, appears from what follows in the same verse as to labouring in word and doctrine. Here then is an explicit mention of presbyters as rulers in the church, without any reference to a superior human power. Where shall we find an equally distinct ascription of the ruling power to Apostles, not of the original thirteen? If here, as in the case of πρεσβυτέριον, it should be said, that πρεσβύτεροι means Apostles, then, besides that the assumption is entirely gratuitous, Timothy, according to the adverse doctrine, was a hyper-apostolical church-officer, not only equal but superior to Paul, who was a mere Apostle.

"Against an elder receive not an accusation but before two or three witnesses," i. e. upon their testimony (1 Tim. 5:19). If πρεσβύτερος here means a ruling elder, as distinguished from a preacher, this is nothing more than a direction to a pastor with respect to charges brought against his assessors. But granting that the word is here to be taken in its highest sense, what does this verse prove, as to Timothy's relative position, with respect to these presbyters? Simply this, that he was empowered to "receive an accusation" against them. There is nothing said of punishing, condemning, nor even of trying them. The only act mentioned is that of receiving an accusation against them. For any thing that appears, the reference might be merely to accusations of a private kind, which Timothy is cautioned not to "receive" without satisfactory proof. But even granting that the reference is clearly to judicial process, it will only prove that Timothy had power to judge presbyters. From this some argue that, in judging presbyters, he held an office superior to theirs. Let us grant, for a moment, that he did; this superior office may have been a temporary one. The most that can with reason be inferred is that a presbyter was sometimes clothed with extraordinary powers to try other presbyters. Nor is there any thing unnatural or contrary to analogy in this hypothesis. The favourite privilege of modern freemen is to be tried by their peers. If an Apostle, or "Apostle-bishop," were accused, by whom would he be tried? By one or more of the same order. Would it follow from this that the judges were superior to the accused in permanent official rank? There is no distinction between the cases arising from the fact that Timothy alone is mentioned. Admitting that the fact is so, although it may be customary, and on the whole desirable, to appoint a plurality of judges in such cases, there is nothing absurd in the appointment of a single one. Some jurists have contended for such a constitution of all courts as the most safe and reasonable. It is not asserted that Timothy was clothed with this extraordinary power. It is only asserted that this is quite as fair an inference from the proposed interpretation of the verse before us, as the inference that Timothy must have had a permanent office above that of presbyter, because he acted as the sole judge of presbyters.

But what proof is there that he was to be the sole judge? It has hitherto been granted, in order to evince that, even in that case, nothing could be proved as to his holding a superior rank. But the concession was entirely gratuitous. It rests on nothing but the fact that Paul's instructions are addressed to Timothy in the second person singular, "Receive not THOU an accusation." Let us see what would follow from the rigid application of this rule. If the singular form of the command in question proves that Timothy alone was to receive accusations against Presbyters, then the similar form, used in other parts of the epistle, proves that he alone was to war a good warfare, holding faith and a good conscience (ch. 1:18, 19); that he alone was to refuse profane and old wives' fables, and exercise himself rather unto godliness (ch. 4:7); that he alone was to command and teach these things (ch. 4:11); that he alone was to be an example of the believers in word, in conversation, in charity (ch. 4: 12); that he alone was to give attendance to reading, to exhortation, to doctrine (ib. v. 13); that he alone was to meditate upon these things and give himself wholly to them (ib. v. 15); that he alone was to take heed unto himself and to his doctrine, and to continue in them (v. 16); that he alone had hearers, whose salvation or perdition was at stake (ib.). Is it valid reasoning to infer from these commands that Timothy was the only preacher in Ephesus? If so, where were his presbyters? If not, why should the personal address, in ch. 5:19, prove any thing more, as to the limitation of the powers and duties there referred to, than it does in all the other cases above cited? If it be asked, who else could be included in the exhortation, the answer is, they who held the same office, or the Presbyters mentioned in the context. It is not necessary for my present purpose to allege that this must be the meaning. It is sufficient to maintain that it may be, and that consequently there can be no just ground for assuming that the official acts ascribed to Timothy were exclusive acts.

If it be asked, why he is individually addressed, and not as one of a number, it is a sufficient answer, that Paul was writing to him alone, and that the acts to be performed were individual acts, whether performed in conjunction with others or not. If an English Bishop should address a letter to an American one, advising him as to the performance of his duties, might he not naturally say to him, "I hope my brother will be careful, both as to the persons whom he admits to the episcopal office, and as to the reception of charges against them, when they are admitted?" Would it be fair to infer from this that the person addressed had the sole right of consecrating bishops and of trying them? Would not the inference be at least as fair, that what was said to him individually had respect to functions which could only be performed in conjunction with others? And if so, may we not infer the same thing in the case of Timothy? The bare possibility of such an inference makes it at least unnecessary to infer, that because Timothy is individually addressed, he alone was competent to do the acts commanded. No doubt multudes of letters have been written to young Presbyterian ministers, in which the same form of address was used in reference to acts which, according to our constitution, no presbyter can ordinarily perform alone. If then Timothy is not here mentioned as the sole judge of accused presbyters, nothing can be inferred as to his superiority. If, on the other hand, he is so mentioned, it is more natural to infer that he was clothed with an extraordinary judicial power, than that he held an office which he is nowhere said to have held, by the name of which he is nowhere called, and the very existence of which, as a part of the permanent church-system, is a matter of dispute.

The fallacy of the adverse reasoning may be made apparent by an illustration. Suppose a letter should be found hereafter, addressed to an officer in our navy, and advising him as to his conduct respecting certain accusations brought against a captain in the same service, the address throughout being singular in its form, and without any intimation of its being applicable to any other person. Suppose this passage to occur in the letter, "I would advise you never to receive a charge against a captain without ample proof." A writer on naval history infers from these expressions, that they relate to judicial process; that the person addressed had the sole right of trying the accused; and that he must therefore have been superior in rank to a post-captain. Subsequent inquiry shows, perhaps, that the language of the letter related merely to private accusation; or if not, that the person addressed was one of a Court Martial, and in rank precisely equal to the accused party. Are not the supposed words perfectly consistent with this state of the case? If so, what follows as to the nature of the reasoning, which led to the false conclusion? That it proves nothing, because it proves too much. If, now, this reasoning had been used to prove that the rank of Admiral existed in the United States Navy in 1850, would it not very much resemble that which is used to prove that Apostles (not of the original thirteen) existed in the primitive church? That argument, so far as it is founded on this passage, takes for granted, that the words relate to judicial process against presbyters; that Timothy is represented as the sole judge; and that he could not be so unless superior to presbyters in permanent official rank. Waving the first point, or admitting its correctness, it may be alleged, in opposition to the second, that he need not be supposed to have been the sole judge; and to the third, that his judging presbyters, whether alone or not, is no proof that he was more than a presbyter himself. Indeed, supposing presbyters, as we do, to have been the highest permanent officers in the church, it was only by presbyters that they could be tried, just as in the Protestant Episcopal Church bishops must be tried by bishops, and in the army generals by generals. Whether Timothy tried presbyters by virtue of extraordinary powers, or in the discharge of his ordinary duties as a member of a presbytery, matters not. Either of these suppositions sufficiently accounts for the expressions in the text, and thereby precludes the necessity of assuming a permanent superiority of rank. He is elsewhere described as a presbyter; he is nowhere described as an apostle; what he was here described as doing he was competent to do as a presbyter; it is therefore unreasonable to infer that he was an apostle.

The same remarks apply to ch. 5:22. "Lay hands suddenly on no man, neither be partaker of other men's sins." It may even be questioned, whether this relates at all to ordination. Why may it not refer to the gift of the Holy Spirit? If such a reference is even supposable in ch. 4:14, it is highly probable in this place, where nothing is mentioned but the bare imposition of hands. But granting that it does refer to ordination, it is not said to what office; and why may it not have been to that of deacon? But even granting that it refers to the ordination of presbyters, it does not follow, for the reasons above given, that Timothy alone was to lay on hands. And if he did it alone, he may have done so merely as a presbyter, or by virtue of an extraordinary but temporary power. A solitary

Presbyterian minister, under certain circumstances, might ordain others, in perfect consistency with Presbyterian principles. Whether Timothy was clothed with extraordinary powers, for a particular occasion, matters not. If he was the only Presbyter in Ephesus, the necessity of the case would authorize him to ordain. The requisition of a plurality is not to be found in Scripture. The principle involved in ordination is that it can only be performed by one who has himself been ordained. And this requisition is as really complied with by the act of one ordainer as by that of twenty. For obvious reasons of expediency, the exercise of the power may be limited, in ordinary cases, to a plurality of persons; but the restriction rests upon no principle. If one bishop in the Protestant Episcopal Church can admit others to an order inferior to his own, there is no reason, except usage and arbitrary regulation, why he should not, if necessary, admit one to the same office which he holds himself. Even supposing, then, that Timothy ordained alone, it does not follow that he was superior in rank to Presbyters. The Apostle's exhortation would be perfectly appropriate, if addressed to one of a body of Presbyters. And we know from Acts 20: 17, that there were other Presbyters in or about Ephesus. The assumption, then, that Timothy held an office superior to that of Presbyters, is wholly unsupported by the text before us.

In 1 Tim. 6: 2, Timothy is commanded to teach and exhort servants as to their relative duties. In the next verse, Paul denounces any who should teach otherwise, implying that there were others authorized to teach. This passage, then, relates to powers which

Timothy possessed in common with others. From such false teachers he is commanded to withdraw himself. This could hardly be addressed to an ecclesiastical superior, who possessed the sole right of exercising discipline. It applies much better to one among a number of authorized teachers, whose defence against them was to shun their company. In v. 11, the Apostle exhorts Timothy to avoid the sin of covetousness, and to cultivate the Christian graces, to fight the good fight of faith, and to lay hold of eternal life. He speaks of him, at the same time, as having "professed a good profession." This commandment he charges him to keep "without spot, unrebukable, until the appearing of our Lord Jesus Christ" (vs. 13, 14). This must refer to the immediately preceding exhortation, as to the seeking of salvation, and the cultivation of the Christian graces. It cannot, therefore, be used as an argument to prove that Timothy had not a temporary commission of an extraordinary kind. In vs. 17–19 Paul tells him what exhortations he should give to rich men. In v. 20 he charges him to be faithful to his trust, and on his guard against a spurious philosophy. All these advices are perfectly appropriate, if addressed to a mere Presbyter.

The second epistle is addressed by "Paul an Apostle of Jesus Christ," to Timothy, not as a brother-apostle, but as a "dearly beloved son." Such an address would certainly not have been unnatural, even to an official equal, much inferior in age. But it cannot be denied that the continual omission of the apostolical title, in the very places where we might expect it, is somewhat unfavourable to the truth of the position, that Timothy was a "supreme Apostle." In the sixth verse, Paul says, "Wherefore I put thee in remembrance, that thou stir up the gift of God which is in thee by the putting on of my hands." This relates either to the gift of the Holy Ghost or to ordination. If the former, it proves nothing as to Timothy's official rank, since persons not described as ministers at all sometimes conferred the Holy Ghost, as appears from the case of Ananias, Acts 9:17. If it relates to ordination, it must have been either to the deaconship, the eldership, or the apostleship. The first has never been alleged. If it was to the eldership, the same transaction is referred to as in 1 Tim. 4:14, from which, as we have seen, it may be proved that presbyters ordained. Or even granting that the ordination was performed by an Apostle, if it was to the office of a presbyter, Paul's twice exhorting him to stir up the gift conferred upon him in his ordination to the eldership, strongly implies that he was nothing more, and indeed that this was the highest permanent office in the church. If, on the other hand, the ordination spoken of is to the office of Apostle, then it follows that Timothy received this ordination in the interval between the two epistles, and, consequently, that the powers ascribed to him in the first epistle (including those of discipline and ordination) belonged to him as a presbyter. The same remarks apply to v. 14, "that good thing which was committed unto thee, keep by the Holy Ghost which dwelleth in us." In v. 13, Timothy is exhorted to hold fast "the form of sound words" which he had heard from Paul, who still addresses him as his pupil and inferior, without the least allusion to his being a colleague and "supreme Apostle."

Ch. 2:1. "Thou therefore, my son, be strong in

the grace that is in Christ Jesus; and the things that thou hast heard of me among many witnesses, the same commit thou to faithful men who shall be able to teach others also." Timothy is here directed to ordain teachers. From this some infer that he held an office superior to that of Presbyter. But this assumes, first, that he was to ordain alone, and then, that a person cannot be admitted to a given rank, except by one who holds a higher rank. The first, as we have seen, is a gratuitous assumption. The second would render it impossible to perpetuate the highest order. If an Apostle could ordain Apostles, it is not to be assumed as an impossibility that a Presbyter should ordain Presbyters. How can it be argued that, because Timothy ordained Presbyters, he must have been more than a Presbyter himself, any more than that because Paul (according to the adverse theory) ordained Apostles, he must have been something more than an Apostle? If the latter conclusion does not follow of course, neither does the former. If an Apostle could ordain Apostles, the natural presumption (in the absence of all proof to the contrary) is that Presbyters could ordain Presbyters. This would be a natural presumption, even if the perpetuity of the apostolic office could be proved. How much more when the antecedent probabilities are all against it, and when this very text is relied upon, as one of the few passages which prove it. The question is whether peculiar apostolic powers are ascribed to Timothy. The proof of the affirmative is, that he ordained Presbyters. The very same fact we adduce as proof that Presbyters ordained. If we have no right to assume that he acted as a Presbyter, still less right have our opponents to assume that none except Apostles ordained. We know that Timothy was a Presbyter, but we do not know that he was an Apostle. It is, therefore, more allowable to assume that Timothy ordained as a Presbyter, which we know him to have been, than that he ordained as an Apostle, which we do not know him to have been.

In this same chapter, Paul exhorts Timothy to endure hardness (v. 3), to consider what he heard or read (v. 7), to put the people in remembrance of these things, charging them before the Lord that they strive not about words to no profit (v. 14). "Study to show thyself approved unto God, a workman that needeth not to be ashamed, rightly dividing the word of truth, but shun profane and vain babblings, for they will increase unto more ungodliness" (vs. 15, 16). How much more natural and appropriate are these advices, if addressed to a mere Presbyter, than if addressed to a "Supreme Apostle;" and how strange is it that among these exhortations, having reference to the duties of a Presbyter, not one should have crept in, relating to any peculiar apostolic function. How strange that Paul should have nothing to say to his brother-apostle about apostolic powers and duties, while he exhorts him to "flee youthful lusts" (v. 22), to "follow righteousness, faith, charity, peace," etc. (v. 22), to "avoid foolish and unlearned questions" (v. 23). Instead of telling him what a Supreme Apostle ought to be, he tells him that "the servant of the Lord must not strive, but be gentle, apt to teach," etc. (v. 24). It may be said, indeed, that many of these advices have respect to common Christian duties, and that it might as well be argued that Timothy was a private Christian, as that he was a mere Presbyter. And so it might, if there were not mingled with these exhortations to common duties, some which clearly and confessedly relate to those of Presbyters. But as there are none which indubitably recognize Timothy as an Apostle, the cases are not parallel.

In ch. 3 : 14, after describing the false teachers and seducers, who were to be looked for, Paul exhorts Timothy, not, as might have been expected on the opposite hypothesis, to interpose his apostolical authority, but to continue in the things which he had learned, knowing of whom he had received them. And on what ground does he exhort him so to do? Not because he was an Apostle, but because he had fully known Paul's doctrine, manner of life, etc. (vs. 10, 11), and because he had himself from a child known the holy Scriptures, which were able to make him wise unto salvation, and which were given that the man of God might be perfect, thoroughly furnished unto all good works (vs. 15–17). Here again the most tempting opportunities of mentioning Timothy's apostolic rank, and insisting on his apostolic duties, are neglected. This is still more strikingly the case in the last chapter, where, in view of his own approaching death, the Apostle exhorts Timothy to a faithful and diligent discharge of duty. Here, if anywhere, something might be looked for which should set at rest the question of Timothy's official superiority to the Presbyters at Ephesus. But what are the exhortations given him? To preach the word, to reprove, rebuke, and exhort, to be watchful, to endure afflictions, and to do the work of an EVANGELIST (ch. 4 : 5).

This last word has been taken in a twofold sense. Some suppose it to denote a presbyter clothed with extraordinary powers, for a limited time and a specific purpose. Others understand by it a *preacher* indefinitely, without any reference to his official rank. The former supposition, though perhaps incapable of demonstration, is far more probable, and in better keeping with the tenor of the New Testament, than the supposition that Timothy was an Apostle. If adopted, it explains completely why he was commissioned to ordain alone (as alleged by our opponents) and to discipline presbyters. But let it be granted that the word means nothing more than *preacher of the gospel:* it only furnishes another instance of the extraordinary fact, that every title and description, which could be applied to Timothy, seems to have come into the mind of Paul more readily than that of Apostle, which he seems indeed to have strangely forgotten, not only as respects the word, but the thing which it denotes. However then we may explain the word *evangelist*, it favours our conclusion. If it means nothing more than a *preacher*, it indirectly strengthens our presumption that Timothy was no Apostle. If it means an extraordinary temporary officer, it precludes the necessity of supposing that he was more than a presbyter, even on the supposition that he exercised more than presbyterial powers.

In ch. 4 : 9, Paul commands Timothy to come to him as soon as possible; and in v. 21 he fixes the time, before which he wishes him to come. The reason which he gives is that Demas, Crescens, Tychicus, and Titus had left him. Luke was the only attendant or ὑπηρέτης who still continued with him. Does not this imply that Timothy was wanted to supply their place? This is rendered still more probable by the direction which is added in v. 11. "Take Mark and bring him with thee, for he is profitable to me εἰς διακονιαν, i. e., as a διάκονος, in which capacity both Mark and Timothy had travelled with Paul before, as we have seen. With this, too, agrees the subsequent direction, as to the cloak and parchments, from which of course nothing can be proved as to Timothy's official rank, but which, by a vast majority of readers, must be seen to agree better with the supposition of his inferiority than with that of his equality. And thus at the close of Paul's last epistle to Timothy, we find the latter acting in the same capacity as when he first appeared in history, namely, that of a personal attendant upon Paul, and subject to his orders. He is here recalled as one who had been absent on a temporary service. This serves to corroborate the conclusion that, if Timothy did exercise powers above those of presbyters, it was by virtue of a special commission.

Titus is not mentioned in the Acts of the Apostles. In the second epistle to the Corinthians, his name occurs nine times, in one of which places Paul calls him "my brother" (2 Cor. 2 : 13), and in another, "my partner and fellow-labourer concerning you," i. e. the Corinthians (8 : 23). In the seventh chapter, he is three times spoken of, as having cheered Paul by joining him in Macedonia (v. 6), and by the good account which he gave of the Corinthian Christians (v. 13), and as one who felt a peculiar interest in their welfare (v. 15). In the twelfth chapter he is again mentioned (v. 18) as a messenger from Paul to the Church at Corinth. In Galatians he is incidentally referred to (ch. 2 : 1, 3) as having accompanied Paul and Barnabas on a visit to Jerusalem. In 2 Tim. 4 : 10, as we have seen already, Titus is said to have left Paul and gone into Dalmatia. In none of these cases is there any thing to indicate that Titus was superior in rank to presbyters, the proof of which, if it exist at all, must be derived from Paul's epistle to himself.

In the title of that epistle, Titus is addressed, not as an Apostle, but as Paul's "own son after the common faith," and as one whom he had left in Crete, to regulate *τὰ λείποντα*, the things which Paul himself had left undone. One of his duties is particularly mentioned, that of ordaining presbyters in every city (v. 5.) From this some infer, as in the case of Timothy, that Titus held an office superior to that of presbyter. Now let it be observed that no other proof of this is even alleged. The truth of the allegation, therefore, rests on the assumption that a presbyter, as such, could not ordain, which is the very point in controversy. There is no proof that Titus was more than a presbyter, unless we are forced to infer it from the fact that he ordained. But how can such an inference be necessary, when we may suppose that he ordained as a member of a presbytery, or as an evangelist, by virtue of a special commission? It is not asserted that he must have done so, but merely that he may have done so, and consequently that his ordaining presbyters does not of itself prove that he was an Apostle. Since, then, we are as much entitled to assume that presbyters ordained, as that Titus was not a mere presbyter, let the question between us be determined by inquiring which hypothesis agrees best with the whole drift and tone of the epistle. Is Titus spoken of in such a manner as would naturally lead us to regard him as Paul's official equal and a "supreme Apostle," or as his inferior, subject to his orders, and with no permanent rank or authority above that of a presbyter?

After giving the qualifications of presbyters or bishops (Tit. 1: 6–9), which are the same as those prescribed to Timothy (1 Tim. 3: 2–7), Paul exhorts Titus to rebuke "gainsayers," "unruly and vain talkers and deceivers;" to "rebuke them sharply that they may be sound in the faith" (vs. 9–13). This any presbyter was competent to do. In opposition to such, he commands Titus (ch. 2: 1) to "speak the things which become sound doctrine," and especially to urge upon the different classes of the people their relative duties (vs. 2–6). These things he was to teach, not only by precept but example (v. 7), "in all things showing thyself a pattern of good works, in doctrine showing uncorruptness, gravity, sincerity, sound speech that cannot be condemned, that he that is of the contrary part may be ashamed, having no evil thing to say of you" (v. 8). There is not a duty here enumerated which is not incumbent, at the present moment, upon every Christian presbyter. The same is true of the concluding exhortation in this chapter (v. 15), "these things speak and exhort and rebuke with all authority; let no man despise thee." The only way in which these counsels can be made to have any bearing upon Titus's apostolical dignity, is by assuming that the persons whom he was to teach, rebuke, etc. were all presbyters. Not only is there no intimation of this fact, but the contrary is evident from the whole context, in which the subjects of this discipline are particularly mentioned, not as elders in the church, but as aged men and women (ch. 2: 2, 3), young men and women (4–6), servants (9, 10), etc. The same thing is true of the directions in the last chapter, where Titus is commanded to affirm constantly the duties of life and the doctrines of grace (v. 8), but exhorted to avoid foolish questions and genealogies and contentions and strivings about the law, as unprofitable and vain (v. 9). All this would be perfectly appropriate, if addressed to any presbyter.

Titus 3: 10. "A man that is an heretic after the first and second admonition reject." The power to judge heretics is certainly ascribed to Titus; but in what capacity? Our opponents say, in that of an apostle; we say in that of a presbyter. The only ground of their conclusion is the twofold assumption, that Titus was to be the sole judge of religious teachers; and that he could not judge them without holding a superior office. The same answers may be given here as in the case of ordination, but with still more force, because it is not even certain in the case before us, that any other heresy is meant but that of private Christians. Granting, however, that heretical teachers are specially referred to, and that rejecting them means refusing to ordain them (which is far from being evident), or to excommunicate them; these are acts which, according to the Presbyterian theory, are competent to presbyters, and cannot therefore be assumed as proofs of apostolical authority. The question is whether Titus performed acts which presbyters, as such, could not perform. The adverse party answer yes, for he judged heretical presbyters, and therefore could not be a presbyter himself. We answer no, because presbyters being the highest order in the permanent organization in the church, if judged at all, they must be judged by presbyters.

We have now gone through these three epistles in detail, and the results of the examination may be stated thus.

1. Timothy and Titus are nowhere addressed or described, in Paul's epistles to them, as apostles.

2. A large part of the admonitions and instructions given to them are such as might have been given to mere presbyters.

3. The powers of ordination and discipline are certainly ascribed to them, but without determining in what capacity they were to exercise them.

4. The supposition of an extraordinary commission to these two men as evangelists, and the supposition that they acted as mere presbyters, are at least as probable as the supposition that they acted as apostles.

5. No proof, therefore, can be drawn from these epistles, of the apostolical authority of either.

ESSAY V.

ON THE ANGELS OF THE CHURCHES AND THE FALSE APOSTLES.

Besides the case of Timothy and Titus, an attempt has been made to prove that the apostolic office was perpetual or permanent, from certain passages of the Apocalypse. The first is that containing the Epistles to the Seven Churches of Asia (Rev. 1: 20. 2: 1, 8, 12, 18. 3: 1, 7, 14). The argument founded upon these epistles is, that the "angel" of each church is addressed in the singular number, as if personally responsible for the faith and practice of the church; from which it is said to follow, that each of these churches must have had an official head, possessing exclusively the power of government, and as we know from Acts 20: 17, that in one of them, at least, there was a plurality of presbyters, this official head must have been an apostle or apostle-bishop.

This argument assumes without proof, that the "angels" here addressed were the regular official rulers of the churches, although the word "angel" is employed, throughout the book, in another sense, and although the supposition that they were guardian angels is in perfect keeping with the language of Scripture elsewhere, and particularly in the Book of Daniel, the one which most resembles the Apocalypse. Even granting the probability that the term is here used to denote an office in the church, the necessity of assuming this without proof shows on how precarious a foundation the argument is built. And even if it could be proved, how slight would the presumption thus created be against the uniform tenor of the New Testament, as seen already.

The adverse argument also assumes that these official Angels must have been superior to Presbyters, and in order to confirm this, it assumes that the Presbyters of Ephesus, mentioned in Acts 20 : 17, were officers of one church, over whom the Angel presided as a prelate or diocesan. But we have just as much right to allege, on our part, that the Presbyters spoken of in Acts were ruling Elders, or that they were the presbyters of churches near to Ephesus, or that if there was a plurality of presbyters at Ephesus in Paul's time, there was only one when John wrote the Apocalypse. This last is rendered highly probable by analogy. In our own cities there are churches organized on Presbyterian principles, which anciently had a plurality of ministers, but as the population has increased or shifted, these collegiate churches have given rise to several, each with its own pastor. Now we know that in the planting of Christianity, churches were first established at the central points of influence, from which, by a sort of colonization, others were derived. For obvious reasons, converts in the neighborhood of these mother churches would adhere to them until a separate organization became necessary. Hence the churches founded in the more important cities of the old world would be burdensome charges, and might well employ a number of presbyters, even supposing all such to have laboured in word and doctrine. That there were such presbyters at Ephesus, when Paul sent thither from Miletus, we read in Acts 20: 17. That other churches were derived from that of Ephesus, and that right early, will scarcely be denied. This would leave the mother church with its "Angel," not as a superior to the presbyters around, but as their equal, or at most as a *primus inter pares.*

The personal address to the Angel, then, proves nothing more than the like address, in analogous circumstances, would prove now. Within the memory of many persons still alive, the First Presbyterian Church of New-York had an eldership including three ordained pastors, who alternately ministered in as many places of worship, all belonging to the same church organization. This is a fact in Presbyterian church-history beyond all doubt; but it is equally certain that in the General Assembly of 1842 a minister appeared bearing a commission in which he was described as Bishop of the First Presbyterian Church in New-York City. Now supposing documentary memorials of these two facts to reach posterity, how plausibly might it be argued, that as one man was recognized in 1842 as the bishop of that church, and as it had certainly three pastors half a century before, therefore the bishop in question was a prelate or diocesan, superior in rank to other Presbyterian ministers. The inconclusiveness of this deduction would appear on the discovery, that in the mean time other affiliated churches had sprung up and left the "First Church" with a single pastor, who, according to our usage and our constitution, was styled in certain documents its bishop. Even if the analogy between the cases were fortuitous, it would be a striking one; but when it springs, as we have seen, from a coincidence of circumstances, and the uniform operation of analogous causes, it seems to warrant the conclusion, that a mode of reasoning, which would be fallacious in the one case, may be fallacious in the other. We say *may* be fallacious, for we need no more than this to justify us in resisting the attempt to set up, as essential to the organization of the church, an institution which can only be shown to have existed in the apostolic times by the evidence of passages admitting of two opposite interpretations, with at least an equal share of probability. For the truth is that on either hypothesis (the Presbyterian or Episcopal) this passage may be easily explained, and for that very reason cannot fairly be adduced as decisive proof in favour of either.

The only remaining instance, in which apostolic powers are alleged to be recognized in Scripture, as belonging to persons not original apostles, is that of the ψευδαπόστολοι spoken of by Paul in 2 Cor. 11: 13, "For such are false apostles, deceitful workers, transforming themselves into the apostles of Christ;" and by our Saviour, in his epistle to the church of Ephesus, Rev. 2: 2, "thou hast tried them which say they are apostles, and are not, and hast found them liars." The argument from these texts is, that if there had not been successors to the apostles, there could not have been pretenders to that office. Upon this we make the following observations.

1. The word ἀπόστολος is used, as we have seen, in a plurality of meanings, viz. a messenger of any kind; a religious messenger or missionary; and an

apostle in the strict and highest sense. Now the adverse argument assumes that ἀπόστολοι must have this last sense in Rev. 2:2. And yet it is certainly not inconceivable, that the impostors spoken of may have assumed the name and character of missionaries, or of special messengers to or from the churches. The objection, that such an imposition could not be successful, and that no sufficient motive of ambition or of interest can be supposed, is purely arbitrary, and at least not favoured by the experienee of later times, in which analogous impostures have by no means been uncommon. There is no case of remarkable imposture upon record, the reality of which might not be called in question, on the ground of a strong antecedent improbability.

2. But granting that ἀπόστολοι, in Rev. 2:2, has its highest sense, why may we not suppose that the impostors mentioned actually personated some of the original thirteen? To such imposture the temptations were too obvious to need specification, and addressed to various corruptions of the human heart, the love of notoriety, the love of power, and the love of gain. If it be answered that no like attempt has been made in modern times, for example, to personate the Bishops in this country; it may be suggested in reply, that the facilities for such a fraud are not so great as in the ancient church, and the inducements infinitely less. If, again, it be answered, that at the time when the last of these two texts was written, there was only one original Apostle left, and that one in extreme old age, it may be replied, that as the text in question contains the words of our Lord himself, in commendation of the previous conduct of the church at Ephesus, there

is nothing to fix the date of the transaction mentioned, or to show that the "liars" there referred to were not identical, or at least contemporary, with the "false apostles" of whom Paul speaks in 2 Cor. 11 : 13. Even after the death of an Apostle, his name might be successfully assumed by an impostor for a time.

But, granting that the fraud referred to was not that of personating the original Apostles, but that of falsely claiming to be their successors in the apostolic office, it by no means follows, that they must have had genuine and authorized successors. If a man should visit certain parts of Europe, where America is least known, and there give himself out as a duke or earl of the United States; as soon as his imposture was detected, he would probably acquire the name of the pretended duke or earl of the United States. Would the correct application of this epithet imply, that there were really such orders of hereditary nobles under our constitution? It may be said, that the analogy is not complete, because there have never been such distinctions known among us, whereas all admit that there had been Apostles. Let us then change the illustration, and, to make the correspondence with the ancient case, as our opponents state it, more complete, let us suppose that, while Charles Carroll of Carrollton was the only surviving signer of the Declaration of Independence, an American had palmed himself upon the European world, as one of that famous company. He would have been a pseudo-signer of the Declaration. Would it be a valid inference from this phrase, that there must have been successors to the original signers, and that this man's fraud consisted in pretending to be one of these when he had never been promoted to that dignity? If to this analogy it be objected, that the signers of the Declaration did not hold an office, in which they might be expected, as a matter of course, to have successors, let us, in order to complete the illustration, have recourse to ancient history, and suppose that after the expulsion of the Tarquins, and the introduction of the consular *régime*, an impostor had travelled through the provinces pretending to be king of Rome, or heir-apparent to the throne; and that this impostor had been called, in ancient histories, the pretended king or prince of Rome. Would this have proved that there was really a king, or royal family, in that republic? Surely not; and yet the principle, involved in such an inference, appears to be precisely that on which the adverse argument in this case rests, viz. that the existence of a counterfeit demonstrates the existence of a genuine original.

The fallacy consists in not distinguishing between the absolute existence of a thing *in rerum naturâ*, or its historical existence at a former period, and its actual existence at a given time. There cannot be a counterfeit of any thing which never had a being; but there may be a counterfeit of things no longer in existence, as, for instance, of a coin or medal which has been destroyed. If there had never been ἀπόστολοι, there never could have been ψευδαπόστολοι; but, on the hypothesis (and it is stated here as nothing more) that the apostolic office, as distinct from that of presbyter, was temporary in design and fact, those who claimed to be successors of the twelve, in their peculiar apostolic powers, would be just as truly ψευδαπόστολοι, as if they had pretended to be Peter, John, or Paul. Indeed, the name seems to apply, with greater emphasis, to those who claimed an office which had no existence, than to those who claimed one which was real, but to which they personally had no right. If he was a false apostle who merely forged his own credentials, how much more did he deserve the name, who forged the very office which he claimed to hold.

All this is true, on the hypothesis, that the *false apostles* of the early church were pretenders to the apostolic office as a permanent part of the church organization, claiming to be duly ordained successors of the original apostles. But neither of the suppositions which have been considered, and which Bishop Onderdonk regards as the only possible hypothesis, is so natural as a fourth, which is free from all the difficulties that attend the others. It is simply this, that the false apostles mentioned in the Scriptures neither personated any of the original thirteen, nor claimed to be their official successors, regularly constituted by the rite of ordination, but asserted an independent claim, as original apostles, divinely commissioned just as the first thirteen had been. The frequency with which such pretensions have been made in later times, shows clearly that there may be motives strong enough to lead to the imposture, and that they may for a time have great success. That such men as Simon Magus, Demas, and Diotrephes, might easily be tempted to assert this false claim, and might easily obtain a temporary reputation as apostles, is certainly a natural and probable hypothesis. The only objection is, that such could not have wrought "the signs of an apostle;" those miracles which all men knew to be indispensable credentials of the apostolic office, and that such an imposture would therefore have been hopeless.

To this it may be answered, 1. That the miraculous gifts of the Holy Ghost were not confined to the Apostles, nor even to good men, and that we can easily conceive of their being abused for ambitious purposes, before they were withdrawn. 2. Those who had never received the Holy Ghost sometimes deceived the people with "lying wonders," that is, either juggling tricks, or wonders wrought by a satanic influence, as in the case of Simon Magus. 3. The claim to a divine authority might be maintained among the credulous, without even an attempt to work a miracle, as appears from the case of Mohammed, who was often called upon, by Pagans, Jews, and Christians, to evince the truth of his pretensions in this way, and yet, without compliance, still maintained his hold upon the popular belief. In either of these ways, the false apostles might have obtained credit, for a time, as men directly commissioned from Heaven, to complete or abrogate preceding revelations. And this was the more easy at the time referred to, because the canon of the New Testament was not closed, and the people had, as yet, no reason to believe, that the series of divine communications was at an end. What was thus *a priori* likely to occur, seems to have actually taken place, in reference at least to inspiration, from the warnings contained in the New Testament against false prophets, and the exhortations not to believe every spirit, but to try the spirits whether they were really from God, to prove all things and hold fast that which is good. If the false prophets of the early church pretended to be prophets sent immediately from God, it is natural to conclude that the false apostles made a like claim, rather than that they either assumed the names of the original thirteen, or claimed to be their regular successors in the church by ordination. This being the case, the existence of false apostles, far from proving that the office was continued, only proves that it had once existed.

These are all the passages of Scripture in which, with any show of probability, proofs of the continuance of the Apostolic office have been sought. An attempt has now been made to show, that its continuance is nowhere recognized in Scripture, either by direct assertion of the fact, by a statement of the necessary qualifications for the Apostolic office, by directions for the ordination of Apostles, by the record of their having been in fact ordained, by the application of the name Apostle in its highest sense to any not of the original thirteen, or, lastly, even by the indirect ascription of peculiar Apostolic powers to any not included in that number. Even supposing one or more of these distinct proofs to be wanting accidentally, and the defect to admit of explanation, it is too much to assume that they were all omitted, and are all to be supplied by mere conjecture. It is too much to assume that the office of Apostle was to be perpetuated by succession, and yet that it is nowhere so alleged in Scripture, nor the qualifications of Apostles stated, nor the ordination of an Apostle anywhere recorded, nor the name Apostle so applied, nor any persons represented as exercising the peculiar Apostolic powers. There will, of course, be a difference of judgment as to the question of fact, whether these proofs are thus wanting; but it is surely not too much to assume that, if they are, the perpetuity of the Apostleship cannot be maintained.

ESSAY VI.

ON THE APOSTOLICAL SUCCESSION.

In opposition to the doctrine, that Presbyterian ordination is invalid because not derived from a superior order of ministers, there is a twofold argument, negative and positive. The negative argument is founded on the fact, that there is no order of church-officers existing by divine right superior to Presbyters; that no such order can exist as the successors of the primitive Bishops, for these were identical with the primitive Presbyters; nor as successors of the Apostles, for these, as such, had no successors. The positive argument is founded on the fact, that the primitive Presbyters actually exercised the highest powers now belonging to the ministry.

There is only one ground left, on which the validity of Presbyterian ordination can be called in question, to wit, that it is not derived even from true Presbyters, that is to say, from the regular successors of the primitive Presbyters. This ground has commonly been taken by the advocates for the necessity of Bishops as an order superior to Presbyters. It is through such

Bishops that the succession has been usually traced. The two doctrines are not however identical, nor even inseparable. Even granting what we have alleged—that there is no superior order, and that Presbyters have always rightfully exercised the highest powers now belonging to the ministry—it may still be said that this, at most, only proves modern Bishops to be nothing more than Presbyters, and as such authorized to govern and ordain, but that these powers may not be claimed by those who cannot, like the Bishops, prove themselves to be the successors of the primitive Presbyters.

This argument against the validity of Presbyterian ordination I propose to examine; but before doing so, it will be necessary to define the meaning of certain terms continually used on both sides of the controversy. The necessity of this arises from the fact, that much confusion has been introduced into the subject by the abuse of terms, and by confounding under one name things which are materially different. The substitution of a sense in the conclusion wholly distinct from that used in the premises must vitiate the argument, although the effect may pass unnoticed. Hence have arisen many current fallacies, the popular effect of which has been to give a great advantage to that party in the controversy, by whom or in whose behalf the stratagem is practised. Thus, when the question to be agitated is whether apostolical succession is "necessary" in the Christian ministry, the term employed admits of two distinct interpretations. It may be said to be necessary, in the sense of being convenient, useful, desirable, and therefore binding under ordinary circumstances. The necessity here predicated of succession is an improper or a relative necessity, from the admission of which it would be most unfair to argue the existence of an absolute or strict necessity, as of a condition *sine qua non*, without which there can be no valid ministry. Yet these meanings of the word are easily confounded, or the one supposed to involve the other, so that our theoretical admission of the value of succession, and our requiring it in practice, is regarded as a contradiction of our doctrine that it is not essential, and the seeming inconsistency throws weight into the scale of the adverse argument. The fallacy consists in the assumption, that the utility and relative necessity of this arrangement springs from its absolute necessity, whereas it springs from its simplicity, convenience, and the want of any better method to perpetuate the ministry. If we are bound to effect a certain end, we are bound to effect it in the most direct and efficacious method; but if this method ceases to possess these qualities, our obligation to employ it ceases, while our obligation to attain the end remains unaltered.

The facility with which the two things here distinguished are confounded may be made apparent by an illustration. It is a rule of most legislative bodies, that the qualifications of the members shall be judged of the body itself, and consequently that no new member shall enter upon his functions, until formally recognized and admitted by his predecessors. This practice has been found so useful and is reckoned so important, that with us it is inserted in the Constitution, and in England, whence it is derived, the House of Commons has by solemn votes asserted it to be a natural and necessary right inherent in the body. The historical fact however is that this important power has repeatedly changed hands, and that recently a proposition has been made to transfer it. Whatever may be thought, by those concerned and authorized to judge, of the expediency of such a change, it would evidently not affect the source or tenure or extent of legislative power in the members of the house. The obvious advantages belonging to the present system, and the force of habit and association, may have led men to believe that reception by the sitting members is essential to the legislative standing of one newly elected; but in point of fact, it is derived from a source exterior to the body and independent of it. This is not adduced as an argument against ministerial succession, but merely as an illustration of the statement that a relative necessity may come to be confounded with an absolute necessity, or at least regarded as a certain proof of it.

The same discrimination is necessary in relation to the word "succession," which may either mean an uninterrupted series of incumbents, so that the office is never vacant, or a succession in which the authority of each incumbent is derived directly from his predecessor. The material difference between these senses of the term, and the facility with which they may nevertheless be confounded, will be made clear by a single illustration. The Kings of England and the Presidents of the United States hold their office in a regular succession, equally uninterrupted and equally necessary in both cases. But the nature of the succession is entirely different. Each King derives his kingly office from his personal relation to his predecessor. Each President derives his office from the people, without any action on the part of his predecessor contributing to it, often against his wishes, and sometimes in direct opposition to his claims as a competitor. The former is a derivative succession; the latter a succession of mere sequence. Nor is this the only distinction to be made in the application of the word "succession," which may sometimes have relation to whole bodies or classes of men, and sometimes to single individuals, in which respect it may be distinguished as general or particular succession.

With these preliminary explanations, let us now proceed to consider the necessity of what is called the Apostolical Succession as a condition of a valid ministry. And let it be observed that the amount of evidence in this case should bear due proportion to the extent and the importance of the allegations in support of which it is adduced. If the question were whether an unbroken succession is lawful, or expedient, or an ancient practice, or of apostolical origin, much less would be requisite to establish the affirmative than is required to prove it absolutely necessary to the existence of a valid ministry. When a question of such moment is at issue, it is not too much to ask that the proof adduced be clear, conclusive, and if possible cumulative. Especially may we expect the proposition to be confirmed by an express divine command, or in default of that by some clear Scripture analogy, or, at the least, by clear proof of some natural necessity arising from the nature of the ministry or its design. All these conditions might be fairly insisted on. The want of any, even of the least, would shake the credit of the adverse doctrine, much more the want of several and even of the greatest; but if all are wanting, we must either reject the doctrine or believe without a reason.

To begin with the most important, if not indispensable; where is the express command, requiring an unbroken succession in the ministry? The only passage which can be made to bear such a construction, is that in which Paul writes to Timothy: "The thing that thou hast heard of me among many witnesses, the same commit thou to faithful men, who shall be able to teach others also." 2 Tim. 2 : 2. In order that this text may be made to prove the doctrine now in question, it must be assumed, first, that it relates to a regular derivative succession in the ministry; then, that it makes such a succession absolutely necessary; and lastly, that it makes the succession more necessary than the other things mentioned in connection with it, namely, faith or fidelity, ability to teach, and conformity of doctrine to the apostolic standard. Without this last assumption the argument will prove too much for those who use it, by proving their own orders to be vitiated by a want of ability or faith in any of their predecessors. But all these assumptions are gratuitous. The text speaks only of the transfer of authority to teach from Timothy to others, without mentioning the precise mode in which the transfer should be subsequently made. It is not even said, "who may be able to ordain others also," as might have been expected if the precept were intended to enforce the necessity of an unbroken ministerial succession.

But even granting that it does enjoin such a succession, it does not so enjoin it as to make it more essential to the ministry than many other things which were enjoined by the Apostles upon their contemporaries, but are now regarded as no longer binding. Or if this be conceded, it is surely arbitrary in the last degree to make it obligatory as to this one circumstance of a succession, and not as to others which are mentioned with it. There are four things included in the requisition, the continuance of the office, faith or fidelity, ability to teach, identity of doctrine with that of the Apostles. Now the adverse argument supposes the first of these—and that not merely the continuance of the office, but its continuance in a certain form—to be rendered absolutely and for ever binding, while the others are regarded as mere secondary circumstances. Either no such distinction is admissible between the parts of the command, or if it is, it may be differently drawn. If one may insist upon the mere succession as essential, another may with equal right insist upon fidelity, ability, or soundness in the faith. This last, indeed, may be contended for, not only with an equal but a better right, because the test of doctrinal conformity is elsewhere made essential, which is not the case with that of succession. All this would be true, even if uninterrupted succession in the ministry had been expressly mentioned in the text, whereas it is found there only by inference, so that if we adopt the meaning which the adverse argument would put upon the passage, we are under the necessity of supposing that which is not mentioned here, nor at all commanded, elsewhere, to be more obligatory than other things, which are particularly named here, and especially enjoined elsewhere. If this is unreasonable or absurd, the text in question cannot be a proof of the necessity of an unbroken ministerial succession. And yet this, if not the only text, is much the strongest, that has ever been appealed to, in support of the position. There is no other which has even the appearance of an express command upon the subject.

It is necessary therefore to supply the want of positive explicit declarations, by the substitution of analogies, for instance that afforded by the succession of the Jewish Priests. As these were ministers in the church of God, it may be argued, that the requisition of uninterrupted succession in their case creates a strong presumption, that the same would be required in the Christian ministry. But can it prove such succession to be absolutely indispensable? Such a conclusion presupposes, 1, that the existence of succession in the old economy can be binding upon us without express command; 2, that the only analogy thus binding is that of the Levitical Priesthood; 3, that the succession of the Jewish Priests was of the same kind that is now contended for; 4, that in this Levitical succession, thus obligatory on us, there are some things which we may discard or imitate at our discretion.

Let us look at the ground of these assumptions, and first that we are bound by the analogy of Jewish succession. It will not be denied by either of the parties to this controversy, that the churches of the old and new dispensations were essentially the same. As little will it be disputed that in some points they were extremely different, and that the differences were not arbitrary or fortuitous but characteristic. Now the grand distinctive features of the old dispensation and of the church under it were its ceremonial forms and its restrictions; the stress laid upon outward regularity, and the limitation of the church to one small country and a single race. And as some parts of the old economy were intended to be permanent and others temporary, these must be distinguished by observing whether any given right or usage bears the peculiar impress of the system which was done away in Christ. Let this test be applied to the requisition of an uninterrupted ministerial succession. With which economy does it more naturally harmonize? With that which was characteristically ceremonial, making spiritual interests dependent to a great degree upon external forms, or with that in which the ceremonial element appears to be reduced to its minimum? With that in which, by means of local restrictions, an unbroken succession might be easily secured and promptly verified, or with that in which the abolition of all national and local limitations makes the application of the rule precarious, if not impossible? Surely if any institution or arrangement can be said, in an extraordinary measure, to require and presuppose the peculiar circumstances of the ancient dispensation, the necessity of uninterrupted succession may be so described.

But this is not the only consideration which would lead to the conclusion that the official succession of the Jewish constitution was a temporary rather than a permanent arrangement. There is another reason which deserves attention. The ceremonial and restrictive character of the old economy naturally tended to produce and foster a certain spirit of exclusiveness and overweening attachment to external circumstances. This was, in a certain degree, necessary to the successful operation of the system, one important end of which was to keep the Jews distinct from other nations until Christ should come. But when he did come, this necessity being at an end, the disposition which before had been intentionally fostered was discouraged and denounced. And even while the old economy subsisted, all excess of the exclusive spirit which belonged to it was checked and censured in a manner clearly showing that the institutions out of which it grew and to which it attached itself were of a temporary nature. Of these corrections and rebukes, which run through all the writings of the prophets, we have one remarkable example near the first introduction of the Mosaic system, when seventy elders were selected as the subjects of a special inspiration. "And it came to pass that when the Spirit rested upon them, they prophesied and did not cease. But there remained two of the men in the camp, the name of the one was Eldad, and the name of the other Medad, and the Spirit rested upon them; and they were of them that were written, but went not out unto the tabernacle, and they prophesied in the camp. And there ran a young man, and told Moses, and said, Eldad and Medad do prophesy in the camp. And Joshua, the son of Nun, one of his young men, answered and said, My lord Moses, forbid them. And Moses said unto him, Enviest thou for my sake? Would God that all the Lord's people were prophets, and that the Lord would put his Spirit upon them!" (Num. 11: 25–29). Here we are expressly told that these two men had all that was essential. "They were of them that were written," i. e. designated for this very purpose; this was their external qualification. "And the Spirit rested upon them;" this was their internal qualification. Yet simply because they were not visibly united with the rest, because they "went not out unto the tabernacle" but "prophesied in the camp," the zealous Joshua would have them silenced. The reply of Moses seems to have been designed not merely to check Joshua's excessive zeal for his master's personal honour, but to point out the error of postponing the highest to the lowest evidence of divine authority, and taking it for granted that God could not or would not grant his spiritual gifts beyond the bounds of a certain temporary organization.

A remarkable parallel to this instructive incident occurs in the New Testament. Even in the announcing of the new dispensation, John the Baptist had intimated that the Jewish prejudice in question would be wholly at variance with the changed condition of the church. "Think not to say within yourselves, We have Abraham to our father; for I say unto you that God is able of these stones to raise up children unto Abraham" (Matthew 3 : 9). And yet no sooner was the body of apostles organized than a Judaic spirit of exclusiveness began to show itself, a disposition to regard external union with that body as a necessary proof of authority derived from Christ. "John answered him saying, Master, we saw one casting out devils in thy name, and he followeth not us, and we forbade him, because he followeth not us. But Jesus said, Forbid him not, for there is no man which shall do a miracle in my name, that can lightly speak evil of me" (Mark 9 : 38, 39). Some, indeed, are of opinion that our Saviour intended to express disapprobation of the man's proceeding as unauthorized; but of this there is no intimation in his language, and it seems to be directly contradicted by the words "Forbid him not." On the contrary, he seems to teach distinctly, that the evidence in this case of connection with him was of a higher nature than connection with his followers, and derived directly from himself. To follow them was indeed a strong presumptive proof that they who did it followed Christ; but to work a miracle in his name was a direct proof of the same thing. Christ had conferred the power of casting out devils on his personal attendants and immediate followers. We do not read that he had publicly conferred it upon any others. It was natural, therefore, that they should regard it as impossible for any others to possess it rightfully. But here was a man upon whom Christ had bestowed it nevertheless, and he refers them to the possession of the gift itself, as a sufficient proof that he had so bestowed it. This he could not do without implying that the exclusive spirit, which occasioned his rebuke, was one belonging to the temporary system of the old economy.

From this, and from analogous expressions used by Paul in his epistles, in relation to the same contracted views, as well as from the intrinsic qualities which make an indispensable succession in the ministry peculiarly accordant with the forms and spirit of the old economy, we surely may infer, that the analogy of that succession cannot be absolutely binding upon us, unless enforced by an express command. But even if the mere example were thus binding, its authority must of course extend to all the great theocratical offices, and not to that of the priesthood alone, which was no more a divine institution, and no more a type of Christ's mediatorial character, than the offices of King and Prophet. But in the succession of the Kings there was a breach made very early, as if to warn us not to argue from a uniform custom to an absolute necessity. David was no less the successor of Saul than Solomon of David; and yet in the latter case there was derivative succession, in the former not. This, it is true, admits of another explanation; but as to the Prophets, there appears to have been no regular or uniform succession in their office. The general analogy of Jewish institutions, then, and even of the great theocratical offices, would lead to the conclusion, that an unbroken ministerial succession is by no means indispensable. Let us grant, however, for the sake of argument, that the only binding analogy is that of the levitical priesthood; it is not true that in it there was an uninterrupted derivative succession from the time of Moses to the time of Christ. Not to mention that the line of the succession of High Priests was twice changed during the period of the Old Testament history—which, as we shall see, was by no means an unimportant circumstance—it is notorious matter of history, that after the Roman conquest, the derivative succession of the Priests was interrupted, and the appointing power vested in a foreign government. And yet the High Priests who, according to the adverse doctrine, could not be legitimate successors of the earlier incumbents, appear to have been recognized as such by the Apostles and by Christ himself; for when officially adjured by Caiaphas, acting in that character, he broke through the silence he had hitherto maintained.

But even granting that the levitical succession was in these respects precisely such as our opponents plead for, and that being such it binds us to exact conformity, this obligation must extend to every thing which necessarily entered into the levitical succession. But that succession was hereditary, and must therefore bind us, if at all, to a hereditary Christian ministry. If this conclusion be evaded by alleging, that the hereditary mode of derivation was a secondary circumstance, derivative succession being all that is essential, then the same thing must be true of the succession which is formed upon the Jewish model; that is to say, the only thing essential in our case is a derivative succession; the precise mode of derivation is an accidental circumstance. If so, hereditary succession, though not necessary, must be lawful, and if lawful entitled to the preference, because more ancient and accordant with the Jewish model than the mode of ordination. If it be said, that God has changed the mode but made the principle still binding, this assumes the existence of some explicit revelation on the subject; but if there were such a revelation, there could be no need of resorting to the analogy of Jewish institutions as a ground of obligation.

Again, if one may arbitrarily distinguish between the derivative succession as essential, and the hereditary mode of derivation as an accident, another may with equal right insist upon a different distinction, and discriminate between a mere unbroken series or constant occupation of the office as essential, and a derivative succession or the constant derivation of authority to each incumbent from his predecessor as an accidental circumstance. This analogy then proves either too little or too much, for it either leaves the main point in dispute discretionary, or it invalidates all orders not derived by a hereditary succession from the primitive presbyters. This is the case, let it be observed, even after we have granted that the Jewish succession is a binding example, that this binding power is restricted to the priesthood, and that the succession of the priesthood was a derivative unbroken succession; all which, as we have seen, are mere gratuitous concessions.

It would seem, then, that the argument from analogy is no more conclusive than that from an alleged command; or in other words, that the necessity of uninterrupted succession can be neither indirectly nor directly proved from Scripture. If this be so it must of course be fatal to the adverse doctrine, unless it can be shown that there is some inherent necessity for such a constitution, independent of a positive command, and springing from the nature of the ministry itself or of the ends it was designed to answer. Now it will not be disputed, that the end for which the ministry was instituted is the maintenance of truth and its inseparable adjuncts. But if uninterrupted ministerial succession is essential to this end, they must always go together. If the end can be secured by any other means, the necessity of this means cannot be absolute. To say that a certain means is essential to a certain end, and yet that the end can be secured without it, is a contradiction. If then succession is essential to the maintenance of truth, they must be always found together. But that teachers of falsehood and apostates have been found in the line of the most regular succession, under both dispensations, is an undisputed and notorious fact. Some of the highest papal authorities admit that even in the series of the Popes there have been heretics and infidels. And few perhaps would question that the truth has been *de facto* held and taught by those who were externally irregular and without authority. The doctrines of what is called the Low Church are regarded by some high Episcopalians as a serious departure from the faith; and yet these doctrines are maintained, not only by priests but by bishops in the boasted line of apostolical succession. The opposite opinions, on the other hand, have sometimes been espoused by men in churches charged with wanting this advantage, and before any change of their external relations.

Here then, according to the adverse doctrine, is succession without truth, and truth without succession. The latter cannot, therefore, be essential to the ends for which the ministry was founded. The necessity, if any such there be, must have respect to the continuance of the ministry itself. It may be argued that no positive command is needed, because God undoubtedly designed the ministry to be perpetual, and to this end an uninterrupted succession is absolutely necessary. If so, the necessity must arise, either from something peculiar to the office of the ministry, as different from all others, or from something in the nature of office in general, something common to this office with all others. Now the only thing which makes the ministry to differ from all other offices is the peculiar relation which it bears to God; but this instead of making succession more necessary makes it less so. However indispensable such an arrangement might be thought in human institutions, its absolute necessity would seem to be precluded in the church, by God's perpetual presence and unceasing agency. And as to office generally, that an unbroken derivative succession is not essential to its perpetuity, is very clear from the familiar case, before alluded to, of kings and presidents, two offices which surely may be equally perpetual, and yet in one of them derivative succession is entirely wanting. That a succession of mere sequence is essential to the perpetuity of office, is no doubt true; but to assert it is to assert an identical proposition. It is merely saying that in order that an office may be never vacant, it must be always filled. Since, therefore, a succession of the kind in question is essential neither to the ends for which the ministry was instituted, nor to the perpetual existence of the ministry itself, there seems to be no original necessity, arising from the nature of the case, and superseding the necessity of positive explicit proof from Scripture.

If, in default of all such evidence, the necessity of such succession is alleged to rest on the authority of the church, the question immediately presents itself, of what church? The practical use of the whole discussion is to ascertain what is a true church, by establishing criteria of a valid ministry. To say then that the church requires something as the indispensable criterion of a true church, is to reason in a circle. It is, in effect, to take the thing for granted, without any reason; and to this, irrational as it may seem, there is a strong disposition on the part of many. But let them remember that besides the unreasonableness of such a course, it has this inconvenience, that it opens the door for an indefinite number of precisely similar assumptions. If one undertakes to say, without assigning any reason or attempting any proof, that apostolical succession, in the sense before explained, is absolutely necessary to a valid ministry, another may, with equal right and equal want of reason, insist upon inspiration or the power of working miracles, pretending at the same time to possess them. Nor would this claim be chargeable with any more absurdity than that which we have been considering, but on the contrary admit of a more plausible defence. If for example a follower of Irving, believing himself to possess an extraordinary gift of tongues, should make this the indispensable criterion of a valid ministry, and plead the promise of extraordinary powers to the apostles and to those who should believe, the actual possession of these powers in the primitive church, and their obvious utility as means for the diffusion of the gospel; he would certainly make out a very strong case, in comparison with that of him who pleads for the necessity of apostolical succession. The charge of mere delusion or unauthorized assumption would admit of being readily and forcibly retorted, and indeed no argument could well be used by the champions of succession against those of extraordinary gifts, except at the risk of having their own weapons turned against themselves.

The same is true, in an inferior degree, of many other requisitions which might be insisted on, if once the necessity of proof could be dispensed with. There is therefore no security against extravagant and groundless claims, except in the position that none, however slight and seemingly innoxious, shall ever be admitted without clear decisive evidence, of which we have seen the one now under consideration to be wholly destitute. On this safe and reasonable principle, the failure to establish the necessity of apostolical succession, from the word of God or the nature of the ministry, must be regarded as an ample vindication of our orders from the charge of invalidity. To make assurance doubly sure, however, we may add to this negative view of the matter several positive objections to the doctrine of apostolical succession, in the sense before repeatedly explained.

In the first place, it appears to be at variance with the doctrine, common to both parties in this controversy, that the Lord Jesus Christ is the supreme Head of the Church, and as such present with her to the end of the world. The doctrine of succession seems to rest upon a false and fanciful analogy, derived from human institutions, where the founder, being mortal, loses all control of his affairs by death, and is thenceforth inaccessible, except in a figurative sense, through those who have succeeded to the trust. In them he lives as "in a figure" (*ἐν παραβολῇ*, Heb. 11: 19); and through them his will is supposed to be consulted and complied with. Now in such a case succession is the only link between the founder and later generations. It is indispensable, or may be so in certain cases, only because nothing can be substituted for it. But the church of Christ is no such corporation; for its founder, though once dead, is alive again and ever liveth to make intercession for his people, and as Head of the Church is still within their reach. True, he uses human intervention in the government of his church, that is, the intervention of its present rulers; but to say that his communications pass through all the links of the immense chain which connects the church of this day with the church of the apostles, is to say that he was nearer to their first successors than he is to us; for if he was not, why must we resort to them as an organ or medium of communication?

And what seems especially remarkable is this, that some who plead for the immediate presence of our Saviour's body in the eucharist should deny his spiritual presence in the church, by deriving all authority, not from him directly, or through those whom he actually uses as his instruments, but through a long succession of dead men, reaching back to the apostles, as if Christ had never risen. Thus the popish doctrines of the real presence and of the sacrament of orders, by a strange juxtaposition, go together. The doctrine of succession seems to place the Saviour at the end of a long line, in which the generations of his ministers follow one another, each at a greater remove from Him than that which went before it, and consequently needing a still longer line to reach him. But according to our view of the true doctrine, Christ, as the Head of the Church, may, in some respects, be likened to the centre of a circle, and the successive generations of his ministers to points in the circumference, at various distances from one another, but all at the same distance from the centre of the system. Through those who thus surround him he may choose to act on others who are still without the circle, as for instance in the rite of ordination; but when this has brought them into the circumference, they derive their powers as directly from the centre as if none had gone before them. All valid powers are derived from Christ, and not from the apostles, or from any intervening men whatever. The agency of men in ordination is a simple, natural and efficacious method of perpetuating the ministry without disorder, recommended by experience, sanctioned by apostolical practice, and approved of God, but not essential to a valid ministry, when

Providence has made it either not at all attainable, or only at the cost of greater evils than could possibly attend the violation of external uniformity.

The argument thus drawn from Christ's relation to the church may seem at first to prove too mnch by proving, that the Scriptures are not necessary as a rule of faith, because the author of the Scriptures is still living and accessible. The fallacy in this objection lies in overlooking two essential points of difference between the cases. The first is, that the word of God contains explicit declarations of its own exclusive claim to our obedience, and denounces curses upon any who shall venture to add to it or take from it; whereas the apostles put in no such claim for their direct successors, and utter no anathemas against all others who should claim to be Christ's ministers. The other difference is this, that in the Scriptures there is no succession, as there is in the ministry. The Bible of the present day is that of the first century, and claims the same respect that would be due to the original apostles were they still alive. This total want of correspondence in the circumstances takes off any force, which the objection drawn from the analogy of Scripture might have had against our argument, that the necessity of what is called the apostolical succession supposes Christ to be no longer in reality, but only in name or retrospectively as matter of history, Head over all things to the Church.

Another positive objection to the doctrine is, that a different test of ministerial authority is expressly and repeatedly laid down in Scripture. This is the test of doctrinal conformity, as taught by Paul, in reproving the Galatians for abandoning the doctrine of gratuitous salvation, under the influence of erroneous teachers. (Gal. 1: 8, 9.) That these teachers acted under the authority of a regular external warrant, may be inferred not only from the improbability that such influence could have been exerted by private individuals or self-constituted teachers, but also from the form of Paul's expressions—"if I or an angel from heaven"—which imply that the Galatians might naturally be disposed to justify their change by appealing to the authority of those by whom they were induced to make it. As if he had said, it is in vain that you plead the apostolical commission and authority of these false teachers, for if I myself or an angel from heaven preach any other gospel, let him be accursed. His reproof of the Galatians for their doctrinal defection necessarily implies that it might have been avoided, by refusing to receive the instructions of their teachers. But unless he meant to teach, in opposition to his teaching elsewhere, that they ought not to acknowledge any spiritual guides whatever, his meaning must be that they ought to have applied a discriminating test to those who came to them as public teachers. But what should this test be? The answer to the question is given in the words, "though I, or an angel from heaven, preach any other gospel unto you than that which we have preached unto you, let him be accursed." The form of anathema which Paul here uses, includes all possible degrees of censure; for one who was accursed of God could not be recognized as a member of the true church, much less as possessing authority in it, or entitled to the confidence and obedience of its members. The expressions are so chosen too as to extend to every class of persons whose pretensions could at any time be called in question. He does not say, "if any private individual or unauthorized public teacher"—he does not say, "if any minister, not of apostolic rank"—he does not say, "if any other apostle"—he does not even say, "if any human being"—but by mentioning himself and an angel from heaven, deliberately cuts off all claim to exemption from the operation of the rule. The standard of comparison established is not something to be afterwards made known, but something notorious and fixed already. He does not say, "another gospel than that which we shall preach hereafter"—he does not say, "another gospel than that which is propounded by the church"—but "any other gospel than that which we have preached to you already."

Now if Paul could thus appeal to his oral instructions as establishing a standard from which he had himself no right to swerve, how much more may such a test be now insisted on, when the canon of Scripture is complete, and a curse impending over any who shall venture to add to it or take from it. If Paul himself, or an angel from heaven, preaching any other gospel than the one which he had preached already, must be treated as accursed of God, how much more must any other man, departing from the standard of true doctrine now confirmed and sealed for ever, be rejected as an unauthorized pretender to the ministerial office, whatever his external claims may be. If to this it be objected that a man may be accursed of God, and yet be entitled to respect and obedience as a minister, this can be true only where the curse remains a secret, not where, as in the present case, it is explicitly revealed. That Paul when he says *ἀνάθεμα ἔστω* does not speak merely of God's secret purpose, or of the ultimate perdition of false teachers, but declares the duty of the church respecting them, is evident from the imperative form of the expression, "let him be (treated or regarded as) anathema;" from the irrelevancy of a mere prediction to the writer's purpose; and also from a parallel passage in the second epistle of John, where the same test is established. "Whosoever transgresseth, and abideth not in the doctrine of Christ, hath not God. He that abideth in the doctrine of Christ, he hath both the Father and the Son." 2 John, 9. This might seem to relate merely to God's personal favour, without any bearing upon ministerial authority or standing; but such an explanation is precluded by the practical directions in the following verse. "If there come any unto you, and bring not this doctrine, receive him not into your house, neither bid him God speed," much less submit to his instructions, or acknowledge his authority, in order to avoid which even social intercourse with such must be forborne, "for he that biddeth him God speed is partaker of his evil deeds." 2 John, 10, 11. In these two passages, by different apostles, and addressed to different persons, conformity of doctrine to the apostolic standard is emphatically set forth as essential to a valid ministry, the want of which could be supplied by no external warrant or commission. The apostolical succession, therefore, in its purest form and clearest evidence, can be of no avail without this doctrinal conformity, because the church is bound to treat not only the successors of apostles, but apostles themselves, and even angels from heaven, as accursed if they preach another gospel.

It may be said, however, that although this doctrinal conformity is necessary, it is not sufficient; that the apostolical succession is another test of valid ministrations, and one equally essential; that the rule which Paul prescribes to the Galatians presupposes an external regularity in the official character of those to whom it is applied; and that although it proves even apostolical orders to be worthless without purity of doctrine, it does not prove purity of doctrine to avail, apart from an apostolical commission. But does not the explicit and repeated mention of the one condition, as absolutely necessary, without the least allusion to the other, in the very cases where it was most important to enforce it, for the guidance of the church, and the prevention of pernicious misconceptions—does not this present a serious objection to the doctrine that the thing thus passed by *sub silentio* was no less essential to the being of a valid ministry than that which is expressly and exclusively enjoined? If the early Christians were as liable to suffer from the want of apostolical authority in ministers as from their want of orthodoxy, why are they frequently warned against the latter, but against the former never?

This objection presses with peculiar force on those who look upon external regularity (including apostolical succession) as the great security for truth of doctrine. If Paul and John had thus regarded it, they surely would have urged their readers to adopt so simple and effectual a safeguard, by submitting to the exclusive guidance of a duly sanctioned and commissioned ministry; their failure to do which is as decisive as a negative proof can be, that they did not even think of apostolic succession, as a preventive of the evil to be feared, but thought it necessary to direct attention to the evil itself, as one with which the people must contend directly, and from which they could escape unhurt only by vigilance, a just discrimination, and a timely exercise of private judgment. Let it moreover be observed, that the value of the apostolical succession, as contended for, depends in a great measure on its furnishing a simple and sufficient method of determining who are and who are not true ministers, without the necessity of seeking other evidence or applying other tests. The very fact, then, that another is required after all, and that the worth of apostolical succession, even when it can be ascertained, depends upon the doctrinal correctness of the persons who possess it, makes it not indeed impossible but highly improbable that this external test was ever meant to be essential. The end to be obtained, on any supposition, is the maintenance of TRUTH, in the most comprehensive sense of the expression; and the strongest recommendation of the adverse doctrine is that it appears to furnish a convenient, tangible, and efficacious method of deciding between different opinions, without being under the necessity of canvassing their merits in detail. But what is the practical value of this method, if its application must be followed by an inquiry whether those who can abide this test are apostolical in doctrine also? This is equivalent to laying down a rule, that we are bound to receive as teachers of the truth all who have apostolical commissions—provided that they teach the truth!

An illustration may be drawn from military usage. The design of countersigns or watchwords in an army is to furnish those who act as sentries with a simple and decisive method of discriminating friends from foes. But what if the officer, in giving out the word, should add an exhortation to observe the dress, complexion, gait, and language of all persons who present themselves, and suffer none to pass who are not in these respects entirely satisfactory? Such a direction might be very wise and necessary; but it would certainly destroy the value of the simpler test to which it was appended; for if even those who give the word must be subjected to its further scrutiny, the only advantage of the watchword would be to save a little unnecessary trouble in a few rare cases. Another illustration of a more pacific kind is afforded by the usage of some churches in admitting communicants to the Lord's table by means of tokens, bearing witness to the fact of their having been approved by the competent authorities. If, in addition to this testimonial, an examination of the person were required on the spot, the use of tokens would be soon dispensed with as an empty form. It may be objected to this illustration, that it supposes proof to be required of the very thing which is attested by the token; whereas apostolical doctrine and apostolical succession are distinct and independent tests of ministerial authority. This is true, if apostolical succession is required simply for its own sake or the sake of some mysterious influence, actually derived from the apostles, through the line of their successors, which we have seen to be at variance with the doctrine of Christ's headship. But if, as I suppose will be admitted by most Protestants, the apostolical succession is of value as securing the possession of the truth, then the express command to judge of the pretensions of all ministers directly by their agreement with the apostolic doctrine, makes it highly probable, to say the least, that an indirect method of determining the same thing was not meant to be equally essential as a test, the rather as it is not even mentioned or referred to, in connection with the other.

We have seen already that the doctrine of apostolical succession, as essential to the ministry, proceeds upon the supposition, that it may be clearly ascertained, and that it furnishes an easy and infallible criterion by which to try the claims of all professing to be ministers. Now if this were the case, it would be inconsistent with the whole scheme of God's providence respecting his church, as disclosed in Scripture and verified by history. So far as his purposes are thus made known, it forms no part of them to place the church beyond the reach of doubt or the necessity of caution. There are promises of ultimate security and triumph, but none of absolute assurance and exemption from perplexity in the mean time. On the contrary, the word of God abounds with warnings against error and deception and with exhortations, not to outward conformity as a preventive, but to watchfulness and diligence and nice discrimination. Christians are there taught not to believe every spirit, but to try the spirits whether they be of God; to prove all and hold fast that which is good. 1 John 4:1. 1 Thess. 5:21. "There must be heresies (or sects) among you, that they which are approved may be made manifest among you." 1 Cor. 2:19. This would seem to be a very unnecessary discipline, if the original organization of the church involved a simpler and less dangerous method of attaining the same end. With these intimations of the Scripture agree perfectly the facts of all church history, as showing that the means, by which God has been pleased to preserve and to restore the knowledge of his truth, have not been those afforded by ecclesiastical organizations or implicit faith in certain teachers as successors of the apostles, but others involving the necessity of studying the truth and searching the Scriptures, as the only sovereign rule of faith and practice.

When considered in this aspect, the alleged simplicity and perfect certainty of apostolical succession, in determining all doubts, without the troublesome necessity of reasoning or investigation, far from proving it to be a necessary part of the divine economy in governing the church, would rather tend to raise a strong presumption that it formed no part of it at all, because at variance with its other parts and with its fundamental principles. And this presumption is abundantly confirmed by the fact, which may easily be verified, that no such facility or certainty as that alleged attends the process, but that, on the contrary, whatever it may seem to be in theory, it always must in practice be uncertain and precarious. Now if the apostolical succession, as we have already seen, is not explicitly commanded, and must therefore rest its claims on its necessity or usefulness, and if its only use can be to furnish a criterion of valid ministrations, it is clear that want of safety and efficiency in its application must destroy its claims to be regarded as a necessary part of the divine economy by which the church is governed.

That God has suffered apostolical doctrine and apostolical succession to be put asunder in a multitude of cases, and so changed the condition of the church under the new dispensation as to render it unspeakably more difficult to ascertain a ministerial succession than it was under the old, are cogent reasons for regarding the hypothesis of its necessity as contradicted by the providence of God. And this leads directly to the last objection which I shall suggest, to wit, that apostolical succession, as a test of ministerial authority, is an impracticable one, and therefore useless. The official pedigree of no man living can be traced with certainty to the apostles. This state of the case might be expected *a priori*, from the very nature of the case itself. That every link in the immense chain should be absolutely perfect in itself and in its connection with the rest; that no flaw should exist, in any instance, from defect in the act of ordination or the ministerial rights of the ordainer, through a period of eighteen hundred years and an extent of many nations, must, if looked at without prejudice, be seen to be an expectation too extravagant to be fulfilled, without an extraordinary interposition to effect it, of which we have neither proof nor promise.

The reason that it does not thus strike every mind when first presented, is that the nature of the succession in question is apt to be obscurely or erroneously conceived. Many assume that nothing more is meant by it than the perpetual existence of a ministry and its continuance by ordination. But that this is far from being the succession against which we are contending, is apparent from the fact that it is not the test applied to non-episcopal communions. These are required to demonstrate the validity of their ministrations by an exact deduction of their orders from the first ordainers. That this should be possible could never be expected *a priori*. That it is not possible, may easily be proved *a posteriori*, from the fact that even under the most favourable circumstances, where the line of the succession has been most conspicuous, most carefully guarded, and attended by the most abundant facilities for verifying facts—as for instance in the case of the Roman bishops—no such succession has been proved.

But apart from these considerations, the impossibility of proving a particular succession, in the case of any minister, is tacitly admitted, on the part of those who claim it, by evading the demand for proof, and simply alleging the fact to be notorious. The case of ministerial succession is compared to that of natural descent from Adam or Noah, which no man can prove, but which no man disputes. The fallacy of this analogical argument scarcely needs to be exposed. The descent of any individual from Adam is notorious only on the supposition that the whole human family is sprung from a single pair. This being assumed, the other follows of necessity. If all descend from Adam, so must every one. To make the cases parallel, we must suppose a plurality of races, and a dispute to which of these a certain individual belongs. In that case the appeal to notoriety would be absurd, and in the absence of explicit genealogies, the only proof available would be correspondence in the physical characteristics of the progenitor and his alleged descendants. In the supposed case this might be a difficult and doubtful process from the want of any accurate and authentic description of the ancestor. But in the case of ministerial descent, we have the advantage of a description not only exact but infallible, with which those who claim to be successors of the primitive ministers may be compared with rigorous exactness. Let us suppose that according to the Scriptures men had sprung from two distinct originals, and that these were represented as distinguished by the same external marks which now distinguish Africans from Europeans. If any one should claim to be descended from either of these stocks, and his pretensions were disputed, the nearest approach that could be made to a solution of the question, would be by comparing the complexion, features, form, hair, etc. of the claimant with the like particulars ascribed in Scripture to the father of the race. The application of the rule might be precarious, but without specific genealogies, no better proof could be adduced or would be called for.

This imaginary case affords a close analogy to that of apostolical succession. Certain bodies of men claim to be exclusively descended, by official derivation, from the primitive apostles, and reject the claims of others to a similar descent, upon the ground that they are not able to produce specific proofs of an unbroken succession: and when charged with the same defect in their own orders, they appeal to notoriety, as if there were no room to doubt or question their extraction. But it may be questioned on the same grounds upon which they question that of others, and the only way in which the point at issue can be settled is by comparing the distinctive attributes of those who now profess to have succeeded the apostles in the ministerial office, with the corresponding traits of the apostles themselves. By this test we are willing to abide. We lay no claim to apostolical succession, except so far as we agree with the apostles and the primitive ministry, in doctrine, spirit, discipline, and life. And we consider our opponents as reduced to the necessity, either of submitting to the same test, or of proving in detail their individual descent from the apostles. The attempt to substitute for such proof the admitted fact, that the Anglican or Romish clergy of the present day are, as a body, the successors of the apostolic ministry, is to evade the difficulty by confounding general and particular succession, by insisting on the latter when our orders are in question, and producing the former when their own commission is demanded. This is a virtual admission of the fact, which forms the ground of our last objection, to wit, that apostolical succession, in the strict sense of the terms, and as a practical test of valid ministrations, is impracticable and therefore useless.

If then, as we have tried to show, this doctrine is not only unsupported by express command and binding example, and by any necessity arising from the nature of the ministerial office, or the ends for which it was established, but at variance with the doctrine of Christ's headship, superseded by the surer test of doctrinal conformity to apostolic teachings, contradicted by the providence of God, and practically useless even to its advocates; it is not perhaps too bold an inference from these considerations, that an incapacity to trace our ministerial authority in regular succession, step by step, to the apostles, is no conclusive argument, nor even a presumptive one, against the validity of Presbyterian orders. Here we might safely rest the defence of our ministrations against all attacks connected with this point of apostolical succession; but we cannot do justice to the strength of our position, without exhibiting the subject in another point of view. We have endeavoured to show, that the apostolical succession, which we are accused of wanting, is not essential to a valid ministry. This would suffice to justify our claims, even on the supposition that our opponents possess in the highest degree what they demand of us, and that we, on the other hand, are utterly without it. But we have furthermore seen reason to believe that our opponents have it in a much more limited degree than that which they require of others. This, in addition to the unessential character of the advantage, would at least have the effect of bringing us nearer to a level with our neighbours, still supposing apostolical succession in the ministerial office to be altogether wanting upon our part.

But even this residuary difference between us, with respect to the validity of our pretensions, disappears when it is known that, so far as apostolical succession can be verified, the Presbyterian Church in the United States possesses it, as really and fully as the Church of England. In making this assertion, as in all the reasonings of the present essay, we assume as proved already, that a superior order in the ministry to that of presbyters is not essential to the being of the church, but that from the beginning presbyters have exercised the highest powers now belonging to the ministry. If so, it is through them that the apostolical succession must be traced, and we accordingly maintain that our orders may be just as surely traced in this way up to apostolic times, as those of any other church through bishops. The denial of this fact has, for the most part, been connected with the false assumption that the ministry of our church has been derived from that of Geneva, and depends for its validity on the ministerial authority of Calvin;

whereas we trace our orders, through the original Presbytery of Philadelphia, to the mother-church of Scotland, which is well known to have been reformed with the concurrence and assistance of men regularly ordained in the church of Rome. The principal admixture of this Scottish element, in our earliest presbyteries, was with New England Puritans, among whom only two examples of lay-ordination are believed to have occurred, and whose ecclesiastical system was orignally founded by regularly ordained priests of the Anglican establishment. The proportion of those members, in our primitive church-courts, whose ordination was derived from more obscure and doubtful sources, such as the Welsh and English Independents, was extremely small. Whatever then a regular succession may be worth, we can lay claim to it as far back and as certainly as any of our adversaries.

This fact is indeed so "notorious," that it has been met, for the most part, not with a denial of the fact itself, but with an allegation, that the only apostolical succession in existence is derived through Bishops, as superior to Presbyters. It is the need of something to destroy the force of presbyterial succession, as a fact which cannot be denied, that has occasioned the perpetual and almost universal combination of the doctrine of succession with the doctrine of episcopacy, as alike essential to the organization of the church. We have ventured, however, to discuss them separately, and have thus been led to the conclusion, that the highest powers of the church belong to Presbyters as such; that succession, if derived at all, must be derived through them; and that through them we possess it no less certainly and fully than the church of England or the church of Rome. We cannot indeed show that every link in the long chain has been without a flaw, but neither can our adversaries do so upon their part. Until the Reformation the two lines are coincident, and since that time, the continuation of the series of Presbyters, in Scotland, England, Ireland, and America, is as certain and notorious as that of Bishops. Supposing then, as we of course do, that the rank which we have claimed for Presbyters is justly due to them, it follows necessarily, that no objection to the validity of Presbyterian orders can be founded on the want of apostolical succession; partly because it is not absolutely necessary, partly because we are as really possessed of it as any other ministers or church whatever. When any urge this argument against our ministrations, they assume two facts, both essential to the truth of their conclusion; first, that such succession is of absolute necessity, and secondly; that they alone possess it. If either of these assumptions is unfounded, it destroys the argument; for if succession is not necessary, it matters little who has or has it not; and if on the other hand we have as much of it as our opponents, they can have no pretext for impugning the validity of our ministrations. By disproving either of those two positions, the conclusion is destroyed. By disproving both, it is doubly destroyed, "twice dead, plucked up by the roots."

THE END.

www.ingramcontent.com/pod-product-compliance
Lightning Source LLC
LaVergne TN
LVHW011225110826
845150LV00006B/1548